Theological Adventures

Theological Adventures

Nonviolent Non-sacramental & Relational Theology Interspersed with Personal Stories

Phillip Michael Garner

WIPF & STOCK · Eugene, Oregon

THEOLOGICAL ADVENTURES
Subversive Readings in a Missional School

Copyright © 2017 Phillip Michael Garner. All rights reserved. Except for brief quotations in critical publications or reviews, no part of this book may be reproduced in any manner without prior written permission from the publisher. Write: Permissions, Wipf and Stock Publishers, 199 W. 8th Ave., Suite 3, Eugene, OR 97401.

Wipf & Stock
An Imprint of Wipf and Stock Publishers
199 W. 8th Ave., Suite 3
Eugene, OR 97401

www.wipfandstock.com

PAPERBACK ISBN: 978-1-5326-1830-7
HARDCOVER ISBN: 978-1-4982-4376-6

Manufactured in the U.S.A.   MAY 4, 2017

Dedication

This work is dedicated to the Hopewell Christian Community in Old Hickory TN who are known under the corporate identity of Global Outreach Developments International. I began with them when the ministry consisted of SLAM (students living a mission) and my son's band Unnamed Servant. Gregg's band was touring the South and facilitating the SLAM mission trips. It was during a trip to Africa when my son, the founder of G.O.D. Int'l, asked me to help start a school to serve the ministry. I served as the Dean and Director of the Institute for G.O.D. Int'l from the beginning. I also enjoyed serving as the Philippine immersion trip leader for five years.

Today my students and friends have become a beacon of hope. Their exemplary practice begins by belief in pursuing the reign of God through loving your neighbor as yourself and God with all that you are. Their service to others is a form of worship that surpasses the formalized ceremony of institutional religion.

Whether growing food with bio-intensive farming techniques to feed rural communities, or building homes, or establishing venues for biblical education, or providing support to local elementary schools, or drilling water wells, or training midwives, or sending formerly trafficked women to school, the Hopewell community of friends at G.O.D. Int'l provide practical help and spiritual direction to people in the U.S. and around the world.

Each one of the regional teams that work in TN, India, Africa, El Salvador and the Philippines are comprised of my former students. They are a consistent inspiration for continuing my study of scripture and theology. It is my belief that biblical exegesis and theology are best worked out in affirming communal practice. I mean that the conclusions reached through biblical study and theological development is confirmed by the successful application in a communal setting. Also, practice that brings God into the world through works of love with faith in Christ Jesus results in the formation of theological ideas. Those ideas if true to the Spirit of the Lord will be found to enlighten biblical readings.

A number of the chapters in this book were born of requests by G.O.D. Int'l teachers for me to wrestle with portions of the biblical text. Sitting in the instructor's room and chatting has often sent me home thinking. I am grateful for those times of interaction. My son, Gregg, has also contributed to my theology through our weekly conversations and coffee time. I love you all.

Mike Garner

Acknowledgements

Brandon Galford

I want to give special thanks to Brandon Galford for his editorial aid in producing this book and for his authorial contribution of the Foreword. His critiques on my theological claims and how I present those ideas were invaluable during the writing process. Brandon has excelled as one of my students and serves as teacher of biblical studies at 'The Institute for G.O.D. International', where he teaches students in the U.S. in a classroom setting. Brandon also teaches students through on online courses in Africa, India, El Salvador, the Philippines and the U.S.

Table of Contents

Dedication iii
Acknowledgements v
Foreword xv
Introduction 1
Part One: Nonviolent Theology 7
    Learning to Read Scripture as Instructive for
    Non-Violent Theology 7

Chapter I 15
    Not the God of War 15
        The Dogs of War 15
    The Rules of War 21
        Reading Deuteronomy 20 21
        The Herem (utter destruction) 24
    A Story of Leyte Landing: War, Politics
    and the Generations 26

Chapter II 33
    Heroes, Rebels and Zealots 33
        Samson the Archetypal Strong Man 33
    Korah's Rebellion a Conflict,
    Contrasting Spirit, Word and Law 47
        Introduction 47
        Narrative Setting and Continuity 50

The Violence of Law or the
Spirit of Reasoned Speech 52
An Ecological Hot Zone 56
Conclusion 59
Horror, Zealotry, and Phinehas 61
Preparation for Reading Numbers 25:1-18 61
Setting the Stage 65
Terror and the Vigilante 65
Wrestling with Scribes 73
A Story: Learning Non-Violent Response 75
Courage or Sorrow 76

Chapter III 79
The Absence of God 79
God, Violence, Absence, and
Culpability in Hosea 79
Absence Violence and Culpability 81
Conflicted Again 86
Hope's End is God's Victory 87

Part Two: Non-Sacramental Theology 91
Introduction 91

Chapter I 97
The Love Feast and Communion as a Tool for Unity 97
Table Fellowship 99
The Ceremonial Tool 99
Remembering in light of John's Gospel 101
A Chiastic structure of John 13:1-19 103
Remembering in Light of Passover 104

Killing the Firstborn 105
A Story of Two Worlds: Romancing
the Bridge 109

Chapter II 115
Christian Institution or Christian Community 115
   Christian Communal Values 118
   Civil Law in Church and Community 119
   The Entrepreneurial Community 120

Chapter III 123
Understanding Holiness 123

Chapter IV 129
   God Is 129
      God is a Relational, Redeeming, Creator
      who keeps Covenant 130
   God is Relational 130
   **Reading Psalm 133 in light of Redeeming
   Relationships** 131
      Grasping at the power of Eschatological
      Hope 132
      The Possibility 134
      The First Metaphor 134
      The Second Metaphor 135
      The Blessing 137
   Creation and Covenant 139

Part Three: Male-Female Relational Theology 145
   Introduction 145

Chapter I 149
The Human Condition 149
- Created Equal 149
- Sex and Violence are Inseparable 160
- The Threat of Chaos 163

Chapter II 165
The Liberation of Women as Theological Enterprise 165
- The Relationship of Liberation Theology and Latina Readings of Scripture 166
- The Women of Jesus' Birth and Resurrection 167
- Promises and a Beautiful Heroine 170
- The Growing Faith of Sarai 173

Rahab 175
- Heroine Archetype Exemplar 175
- Rahab 177

A Story: Guardians of Life 179
- The Abuse of Women and the Unraveling of the Social Fabric 179

Chapter III 185
A Story: Meeting Grandpa Pinyon 185
The Subsistence Ethic of the Poor 193
- Experiencing the Subsistence Ethic 193

A Story on Teaching the Rich and the Poor 197
- The Children of Lazarus from Kenya to Cebu ... 197

Lightning and a Wild Man 203
- The Personality and Story of Elijah 203
- Failed Education in the School of the Widow 207
- Jesus and Miracle Workers (Luke 4) 211

A Story of Raw Faith 214
   Earthquake 214
Chapter IV 219
  The Book of Proverbs and Relational Theology .. 219
   Sexual Restraint 221
   Wisdom is a Liberated Female 223
   The Strange Woman 223
   Excursus 224
  The Birth of Lady Wisdom 225
   Proverbs 8 225
   A Theology on Lady Wisdom 227
   Wisdom Liberates Women 228

Chapter V 231
  Living as Male and Female 231
   Sexual Restraint and Spirituality 232

Chapter VI 235
  Relational Theology and the book of JOB 235
   Polyphonic Depictions of Yahweh 235
   The God of the Prologue 236
   Mythical Men 239
   The Almighty God of the Tradition 240
   Job's Despair 241
   Job's Relationship to his Fellow Sheiks 241
   The God of Nature 242
   The God Who Cares 246
   The God Job Needs 246
   Job's Daughters 248
   Conclusion 249

Bibliography 251

Foreword

By Brandon Galford

I first met Mike Garner at a youth conference in Daytona Beach, Florida in 2001. I was immediately struck by his passion for the scriptures. He taught the book of Ecclesiastes in such a way that it came alive. Coming from a theological background that detached scriptural study from real application, his method of handling the text was invigorating. Three years later, in the Fall of 2004, I felt the Lord's call to move to Nashville, TN and join Global Outreach Developments International as a full-time student and ministry participant. Mike became one of my primary Bible teachers.

Mike Garner doesn't simply read the Bible; he interacts with it, wrestles with it, and allows it to speak in a very real way. By asking the tough questions that few are willing to ask, he comes to conclusions that few are willing to hear. Garner taught me how to approach the text by laying aside interpretive bias and allowing the Scriptures to speak for themselves. He challenged my fellow students and me with the reality that Christianity needs people today who are courageous enough to read the word of God like Jesus did, finding in it the heart of the God whose vision for the world transcends what eye has seen, ear has heard, and mind has conceived.

Theological Adventures

Theological Adventures is a timely book. In an age where biblical literalism seems to reign supreme, this book encourages believers to dig deeper into the text. As a student, I've heard Garner condemn the phenomenon of "bibliolatry" on multiple occasions. As a teacher and writer, Garner demonstrates how a literalist reading of the Bible fails to do justice to the God who must be *sought* and *interpreted*. Loving the Lord with "all your mind" (Matt 22.37) requires a mental exertion that is simply lacking in many modern theological circles. It was the Pharisees (Matt 19.3-9) and Sadducees (Matt 22.23-33) who read the Bible in this way. Jesus never failed to challenge and dismantle such simplistic approaches, demanding that people rethink how they understood the text. In similar fashion, Garner regards traditional theological categories as being too confining. God is so much more than our dogmatic lists can capture. He's alive! He's free! *This* is the God I have come to know through Garner's teaching.

In Exodus-Deuteronomy class, I'll never forget how Garner cut through a literalistic reading of the plague narrative – which has typically been understood as portraying a God who hardens the will of his unwitting rival and baits him into destruction – and accentuated those elements of the text that portray God as being remarkably merciful and patient. In Genesis class, Garner helped me to see a God who is intimately involved in the everyday affairs of those who love him. He's personal. He's interested. And he's *good*. In these classes, and many others, Garner would deliver what we students and other members of school faculty would call "sub-sandwiches": profound, multi-layered theological ideas, packed into concise statements. This book is a compilation of many of those same theological conclusions that were so influential in my own life.

In Theological Adventures, Garner addresses some of the more difficult passages in the Bible. He confronts head-on complex narratives and Hebrew concepts, such as *herem*, Phinehas' zeal, and the violence of Elijah. Never one to avoid a challenge, Garner approaches these passages determined to peel back the layers and identify the character of the One who has revealed his goodness in the person of Jesus Christ. Any passage we encounter *must* be read through the lens of the one who is called "the Word become flesh" (Jn 1.14), "the image of the invisible God" (Col 1.15), "the exact imprint of his nature" (Heb 1.3), he who is "at the Father's bosom" and thus "makes him known (Jn 1.18)." To fail to approach the scriptures in this way is Pharisaical. If we cannot allow Jesus' life to change the way we read these texts – even those that seem to claim quite directly that *God* spoke or acted in a violent manner – then we have missed the revelation of God. This is Garner's theological premise: the revelation of God in the life, death, and resurrection of his Son is *the* definitive lens through which *all* scripture must be interpreted.

By applying a hermeneutic of suspicion and treating the text as literature that must be interpreted and not simply ingested at face value, Garner unlocks genuine meaning in passages that seem to portray God as violent. He argues that nonviolence is central to the divine nature. This is not a peripheral idea. "God hates violence" is a quote that I've often heard Mr. Garner use. In every communicative forum – personal conversations, class lectures, books, online articles and blogs, Facebook and Twitter posts – Mike Garner can be found positing this theological assertion: *There is no violence in God*. What we should fear, rather, is our own bend toward self-destruction. This book highlights this reality through and through. Although only the first of three parts in the book explicitly addresses the concept of nonviolence, this theme permeates the pages from cover to cover.

In this book, Garner addresses three key theological categories: Non-violent theology, non-sacramental theology, and male-female relational theology. In the first section, he not only deals with issues related to man's participation in warfare (e.g. Judges 7, Deut 20), but even those passages that seem to depict God himself as violent and vengeful (e.g. Num 16 and 25). What if a close reading of those stories that seem to portray God as commanding violence actually reveals a very *human* agenda? What if depictions of God's angry vengeance are nothing more than glimpses into a situation from which God has "walked away"? What if God has little interest in our religious ceremonies and rituals outside of our fulfillment of the *ethical* meaning that lies (often obscured by religious agenda) at the root of every sacrament? What if many of the major issues in our world could actually be traced back to failure in the male-female relational dynamic?

If you are open to reading the scriptures in such a way that allows God's word to speak to our world today, you'll be blessed by this book. Even if you are content with traditional interpretations of the Bible, this book will stimulate your theological appetite and provoke you to deeper study. Interspersed throughout its pages are autobiographical sections that highlight experiences from Mike Garner's own life. Theology is only of benefit to us if we *live* it. Whatever chapter of life you find yourself in, the stories themselves are sure to bless and encourage you. The theology presented in this book is guaranteed to illuminate, inspire, and challenge anyone who is hungry for God's word. I am confident of this. It is my prayer that God will touch each one of you, even as he has touched me through Mike Garner's theological insights.

Introduction

Theological Adventures reflects my growing commitment to scripture and nonviolence. This book is a follow up to Interpretive Adventures. The book is three parts: nonviolent theology, non-sacramental theology and relational theology. The first part presents the hermeneutic that reveals non- violent theology from violent texts through reading some of the Bible's most violent stories. Non-sacramental theology presents the community model for Christianity in preference to the Institutional model. Male-female relational theology exposes the presence of violence as a product of incorrect male-female relational practices in the human family.

I have interspersed personal stories in relation to the biblical readings and theological writings that form this book. Rather than produce a work that leaves the author as an unknown personality, I have chosen to include stories from my life that connect me to the teachings that I offer.

When teaching biblical studies or theology classes, I have always incorporated storytelling as a part of the learning process. When in a classroom the mixture of the mechanics of biblical studies combined with the imaginative critical thinking of theological thought can be intense for students. This tension is easily addressed by the exercise of storytelling. Storytelling done well is to take others with you on an adventure that you have lived.

The stories included in this work are presented with a few pictures. I am hoping the vulnerability of my stories displays my humanity in a way that makes reading my biblical teachings more beneficial. Like every interpreter, I bring myself to the text: my life and stories come along with me.

The first part of this work is focused on non-violent readings of difficult texts. With each breath my conviction that nonviolence is God's answer to humanity grows deeper into my soul. I have learned that not only is it hermeneutically possible, but that it is hermeneutically correct to read every book of the bible in a way that affirms nonviolence as God's calling to all human beings. I know someone will say 'Jesus is the answer' and I agree because Jesus' answer is, 'Be nonviolent like me.'

Scripture is to be read as both a revelation of God and a thorough revelation on humanity. First, a person must learn to read the canon through the interpretive method of narrative continuity. Narrative continuity is the acceptance of the canon of scripture as a single book. Narrative continuity does not treat incongruity between texts as a problem; rather the text tends to challenge accepted norms for furthering revelation. I have attended to helpful methods such as a hermeneutic of suspicion that understands scripture to be subversive, undoing the order of the present to reveal the kingdom of God. Other lenses include choosing a compassionate reading over a legal reading.

In an effort to develop a cognitive field of hermeneutics, I propose treating hermeneutics like a toolbox. The toolbox is made up of three categories: methods, literary tools, and lenses. For example, methods include:

redaction criticism, reader response criticism, textual criticism, form criticism, historic-grammatical criticism, etc. Literary tools include the identification of genre, inclusio, chiasm, poetry, narrative, etc. Interpretive lenses include the following; feminist reading, philosophical theology, liberative readings etc.

The value of any reading of scriptural teaching is determined by how it promotes awareness of reality in relation to both God and humanity and contributes to the Spirit's work to conform a person to the image of God in Christ Jesus.

I have for a long time pursued a holistic reading of the Bible. This has required a lot of time, study, thought, education and experience. Along the way I came to the conviction that as a book proclaimed by so many to be the 'word of God', the book is self-authenticating as a word above every word, written or spoken. Rather than depend upon recognizing church authority for the canon, I credit the providence of God. I prefer to understand that the 'word of God' is in particular the *kerygma* (proclamation) received by those that hear, and suggest that it is best to refer to the bible as 'scripture'. As a collection, the Bible addresses human reality and contains the revelation of God in such a way that all humanity's behavior and socio-political efforts are exposed as lacking; only surrendering to the good news of Jesus' teaching and revelation of God can heal our blindness.

When reading a text within any biblical book, I identify the guiding interpretive lens that I use. For example, I read Joshua as a conquest narrative, similar to but more than America's attempt to justify her beginnings. I read Judges in multiple ways, but in particular as a teaching on society's decline, accompanied by the oppression of the feminine voice. I read Obadiah as a record of national hate speech in the name of religion, not God. Jeremiah is a practitioner of non-violence, an instructor for spirituality without national symbols. I find theology based upon skilled interpretation to be an essential and applicable voice, able to cross over technology's progress and bring the ethics of God, even God, into the world.

The second part of this work explores a few texts and offers some thought on the validity of non-sacramental theology and life. I have lived a non-sacramental life for some time. It is better to teach with words and example than through ceremony and symbol. The third and final part of this book explores relational theology, in particular, the male-female relationship and the human relationship with God.

READINGS

IN

NONVIOLENT THEOLOGY

Part One:

NONVIOLENT THEOLOGY

Learning to Read Scripture as Instructive for Non-Violent Theology

Christianity has always existed in exemplary saints, people who refuse to tolerate the status quo; people whose innovative readings of scripture reach back to the Spirit of Christ revealed in the person and teachings of Jesus. Imagine the intellectual commitment to truth exemplified in Jesus' refusal to be bound by the limitations of the interpretive traditions of his nation's religious leaders. Imagine being a person whose readings of 'the writings' are consistent with the greatest teachers and prophets, yet often original (as they were).

Religious people like to define, limit and regulate readings of scripture, according to established traditions. Freire's complaint against the academy for producing a 'banking concept' of education that identifies the learned but resists innovation is applicable to the state of biblical interpretation in Christianity.[1]

---

[1] See: Freire, Paulo. *Pedagogy of Freedom: Ethics, Democracy and Civic Courage* . (Translated by Patrick Clarke. Lanham, MD: Rowman and Littlefield Publishers, 1998) pg 71.

Our institutions for higher education in the disciplines of biblical studies and theology do not encourage original readings. Professors of lesser intellect than a brilliant student can end the student's innovative readings through established expectations and grading. We are now dependent upon the minds of the past to define the world and suppose that any originality must be confined within the boundaries of tradition. Dead men, rather than the Spirit of the Living Christ, often rule us.

An original reading is not merely establishing the validity of a claim based upon recent historical research, though such a reading may be 'new' to the field of interpretive offerings. An original reading is always a theological reading. The original readings of Jesus are theological interpretations that are consistent with historical and cultural understandings of scripture. Further, the theological authorities of Jesus' day could not deny the legitimacy of Jesus' claims and challenges present in his reading of scripture.

What socio-cultural factors would contribute to the development of a personality that reads scripture different from the established norms of academia? How would God be present in the formation of a life that views the world and the scripture different from others? Such questions are entertained in the lives of the prophets and suggest that God uses and calls people from outside the established order. Jeremiah, Hosea and Amos are prime examples. Jeremiah will imagine a new covenant, while deconstructing Israel's socio-cultural and symbolic religious world. Hosea will defy moral expectations for a 'holy man'. Amos is a country boy without credentials, and his intercessions to God on behalf of Israel are granted.

Today Christianity needs people that read scripture like Jesus, like the prophets, people who are not afraid to challenge existing structures of thought with life infusing readings of scripture. These readings will liberate people via theology that wrestles with reality and exposes the ugliness of the 'world'. These readings will not be about the end times or bring recognition and power to the interpreter. The readings we are in need of are those that find God in the Old Testament through interpretive efforts that are consistent with the revelation of God in Christ Jesus on the cross. This is not an impossible task, but it is an imperative task if we are to understand God's clearest revelation of self that is portrayed and defined through the life, death and resurrection of Jesus in relation to scripture.

The redeemed imagination can bring to scripture openness to the understanding of God contained within the stories of the bible. The readings that I am writing about, and thinking of, are not 'folk' readings, but readings that incorporate the best of academic disciplines, disciplines that govern and protect us from presumptuous ignorance or enthusiasm. I think that the greatest need in biblical interpretation for Christian scholars is to interpret the Old Testament through the lens of the cross as revelation of God's non-violent being. If we are to overcome the idols of nationalism, militarism, and materialism, it is imperative that we get past readings of the Old Testament that accept violence as normal, as inevitable or as approved of by God.

Often these readings require some form of demythologization. At times the practice of demythologizing discredits the interventionist power of God at the expense of revelation. At other times it is evident that the text is utilizing the genre of myth as in Genesis 1-11:25. These early stories all have their origin in relation to A.N.E. (ancient near eastern) texts. However, the stories of Genesis 1:1-11:25 are Israel's theology and serve as polemical theological responses to the literary milieu of their time. These stories are proto-historical and provide scriptural claims concerning the human condition and the search for God. They are particularly valuable for anthropological understanding and understanding God's relation to humanity through the created order.

Literal readings of mythological texts results in needless arguments that lose the value of the revelatory theology they contain. Literalism tends to impose on these stories modern concerns or questions that the text was not written to answer. That God exists is a matter of faith and no amount of argument can prove the existence of God. The Bible is a literary work and is subject to the many genres used for communicating in written words. The depth of revelation about humanity and God displayed in the scripture supports the book's authority as self-authenticating.

Writing is a different form of communication than speech. Speech is immediate, whereas writing is subject to careful, time-consuming thought and effort for the production of words. Writing that is meant to be studied, used for contemplative and imaginative purposes regarding God, humanity and creation is subject to use of all the genres and tools that literary artistry provides.

I will provide a simple example of demythologizing that maintains the interventionist power of God into human affairs, while revealing the mythological element. In Matthew 17:14-20 Jesus heals a young boy of epilepsy with the language of an exorcist by rebuking the demon. The story maintains the interventionist power of God to heal the boy, while utilizing metaphysical realities (the demonic) as the cause. I do not think we should lose either claim: that in Christ, God's power has healed a boy of epilepsy, or that at the root of all calamity in the world lies the demonic power of evil; even when today we are provided with science to treat or cure illness.

The personification of evil is a valid form of mythology that serves humanity well when dealing with the unsolvable problem of evil. Myth is the expansion of language into the unknown where science and technological language is bankrupt. Myth alone allows language to transcend time or articulate the unknown imaginatively, but only in part. The myth's of scripture inspire, instruct, challenge, and impact the conscience for living in light of hope that we might rise above the darkness of evil. Ultimate demythologization is impossible for myth is essential to the human creature's spiritual development. Myth and reality are so infused as to be inseparable if we are to do theology. We are creatures of myth and myth is a genre, a form of communication that releases us from concreteness into the life of the 'Spirit' where faith meets God.

The interconnectedness of our lives with all that is in the world and all that has formed and is forming our history is a metaphysical reality. Meaning, our lives generate a power through ideologies and history that seems to have a life of its own. It is a reality easily communicated with mythical language, particularly for the weak (Paul's word for the uneducated).[2]

---

[2] In 1st Corinthian 8 Paul understands that in the conscience of some an idol is representative of an actual entity (demon). These people Paul calls 'the weak' because their understanding of reality has not

The gospel is the good news of humanity's incorporation into the being of God. At present, humanity is viewed by God as a dysfunctional organism of individuals. The unity of humanity can only be accomplished in God. However, we live apart from God's being. God is absent from the creation and the lack that was in the law is met in the incarnation and resurrection of Jesus who reconciles us to our heavenly father. As I am fond of saying,

*God has joined the creation,
and now when speaking of God we must include that
part of what it means to be God is to be human.*

Violence belongs to human beings; there is no violence in God. The eruption of the cosmos in the flood portrays how violence destroys creation. That God lets us live in spite of our violence is the glorious meaning of this horrific myth of destruction. The flood story is an enduring warning of the human potential to resist the voice of God in creation and bring destruction upon our own heads. We need not fear the waters that are present on the earth. Rather, we must fear our own propensity for self-destruction through violence in its many forms. This potential for humanity's self-destruction in relation to the cosmos is the creative design of God. In this sense, God is viewed as responsible for the flood in the biblical narrative. Interpreting reality this way is consistent with biblical wisdom. Wisdom in the scripture is to discern the voice of God sewn into the fabric of creation. Wisdom is always moral, always ethically challenging, and aids us in maneuvering through life with all its challenges.

---

yet reached the place where there is but one God and all other powers are mere constructs for expressing metaphysical aspects of reality.

Jesus has called us to be children of God who bring God into the world through works of love. We are to be peacemakers, servants of humanity who live an alternative lifestyle that brings the flourishing of life beyond the sacrificial progress of science and technology. A world without violence is not mere eschatological hope. It is the everyday calling of God's children to embody. It is for this reason that teaching non-violence in all its subtlety is a spiritual imperative, and exposing violence is an act of spiritual intelligence.

The following few offerings of non-violent readings belong to my efforts to teach that scripture always exposes violence as incompatible with the reign of God in Christ Jesus our Lord.

Chapter I

Not the God of War

The Dogs of War

How to Defeat a Warring People without Violence

Judges chap. 7 is an interesting piece of scripture; it is a lesson in military tactics. In this chapter, God is found in the refusal to use violence. The desire of Yahweh was for Israel not to practice war. That God's desire was for the land to be entered without war is clear in the following passages. However, the tendency to violence and the forming of a professional military is a constant temptation for Israel. God's ways are apparently too slow for Israel and require patience that Israel does not possess. That God is not in a hurry should have been understood through the lives of Abraham and Sarah, or in the life of Moses. We are in a hurry because of our mortality; we live for ourselves, for the moment, rather than with our mortality constantly before us, rather than for the eternal.

> [27] *I will send my terror before you, and will throw into confusion all the people against whom you shall come, and I will make all your enemies turn their backs to you.*
> [28] *And I will send hornets before you, which shall drive out Hivite, Canaanite, and Hittite from before you.*

> ^{29} *I will not drive them out from before you in one year, lest*
> *the land become desolate and*
> *the wild beasts multiply against you.*
> ^{30} *Little by little I will drive them out from before you, until*
> *you are increased and possess the land.*
> *(Exodus 23:27-30 RSV)*

> *I sent the hornet ahead of you, which drove out before you the two kings of the Amorites; it was not by your sword or by your bow.*
> *(Joshua 24:12 NRS)*

Israel fails to learn Yahweh's ways; they fail to trust him and lapse into the idolatry of religious syncretism.[3] In these moments, locusts are not driving out the people of the land. Rather, the people of the land (the Midianites) become like locusts to Israel. The gift of the land is dependent upon Israel's trusting relationship with Yahweh.

> ^{5} *For they would come up with their cattle and their tents, coming like locusts for number; both they and their camels could not be counted; so that they wasted the land as they came in. (Judges 6:5 RSV)*

The driving out of the people in possession of the land includes the possibility of their accepting Israel's God and becoming part of Israel. Israel's exodus and wilderness wanderings included the company of mixed peoples that departed Egypt with them (Exodus 12:38). The inclusion of people in the land is a constant theme in the OT and is revealed in an array of characters like Rahab (Josh 2) and the Gibeonites (Josh 9-10). Israel's greatness was to be her

---

[3] Israel failed to destroy the Asherah and the ideologies of the Canaanites. This failure led to the religious syncretism of Israel's God as compatible with Canaanite ideas of deity.

laws, her ethics for all, both the poor and the foreigner - her faith, not her military prowess and success.

I charged your judges at that time: "Give the members of your community a fair hearing, and judge rightly between one person and another, whether citizen or resident alien. (Deuteronomy 1:16 NRS)

The problem God faces is teaching Israel to trust him, to learn his ways and not become like the other nations, nations that practice war. Judges 7 is an example of God's instructional effort to manage Israel's tendency to war.

Identifying the Dogs of War

Judges 7

Gideon is the son of an idolatrous farmer; however, his father will come to his defense when Gideon destroys an altar to Baal. Gideon's call is marked by his self-perception as the least in all Israel (Judges 6:15). This humility will soon be lost to the grandeur of becoming a national hero.

The story of Gideon's resistance to Baal provides Gideon with enough influence to rally support in an effort to restore Israel's worship of Yahweh (Judges 6:25-35). However, Yahweh's reason for raising up Gideon – or allowing Gideon to rise up –was to re-establish Israel's relationship with God's self. Gideon's call for aid to oppose the worship of Baal results in a gathering of young men prepared to fight. There are always young men who would rather fight than learn a skill and work for a living. Yahweh counters this growing momentum to war with a lesson in peaceful tactics that results in expulsion of the enemy from the land.

Yahweh's resistance to warring begins with a lesson. Israel does not possess a professional military force. Without the conscription and professional training of men into the military cult, without laws to prohibit men from refusing military service, most will choose to go home. So, Yahweh provides a list of reasons for men to go home. Yahweh's complaint is that their number is too large. It is apparent in this piece that the LORD is tolerating Israel's tendency to war and is limiting their efforts to the few persons he cannot stop from warring without using force (violence) to stop them; these few show themselves to be un-teachable, unable to hear the voice of God.

The following verse implicitly states that the LORD operates within some degree of limits caused by human choice.

> *But if you fear to attack, go down to the camp with your servant Purah;*
> *(Judges 7:10)*

The ever present conditional 'if' of relationship between God and humanity results in the acquiescence and instructive reality in the law.[4] God will not let the people win through supreme military force. In a moment of instruction for wayfaring children, Israel must learn this one truth, "God cannot stop a particular segment of the male population from warring". The people will need to teach their children in a way that opposes war as a solution. War as a practice is passed on from generation to generation through the exalting of war stories, making

---

[4] Because law is written to regulate wrong doing it is understandable to say that through the law God acquiesces in order to limit the harm done when humanity will not live up to God's ideals. Moses' divorce laws reflect this truth (Deut. 24) as Jesus affirms (Mark 10:5).

military service an honor to be recognized in society, and supported by the building of state- sponsored memorials.

> [2] *The LORD said to Gideon, "The people with you are too many for me to give the Midianites into their hand, lest Israel vaunt themselves against me, saying, `My own hand has delivered me.' (Judges 7:2 RSV)*

Thinning the Troops

Yahweh has Gideon dismiss all the men that are fearful. Gideon's troops are reduced from 22,000 to 10,000. It seems the lesson is that most men do not want to lose their lives in battle and prefer not to fight. I suspect others desired to go home but were intimidated by the few warriors. Yahweh is displeased with the remaining number and seeks to reduce the troops dramatically. He has Gideon take them to the river to drink water. Those that lap water like a 'dog' are kept; those that kneel down are sent home. Only three hundred men are kept; these are the dogs. The insult is clear; there is no honor in war.

> [5] *So he brought the people down to the water; and the LORD said to Gideon, "Every one that laps the water with his tongue, as a dog laps, you shall set by himself; (Judges 7:5 RSV)*

The LORD speaks to Gideon and tells him the camp of the Midianites has been given into his hand. If, however, Gideon is fearful, he is invited to go spy out the camp with Purah (whose name is derived from the word 'fruitful'). The man chosen by God to deliver Israel is like those that went home first: Gideon is fearful. It is within the literary construction of the text to claim that fruitfulness accompanies those that fear warring. On the other hand, the sending of spies is reminiscent of the other stories of

Israel's need to spy out the land under both Moses and Joshua. Fear and spying out the land is indicative of human effort to expel the people of the land; it is a lack of faith. The removal of faith and the rejection of God from the activity of expelling the peoples in the land allows for a few to be exalted as warriors. The concept of a warrior class has plagued humanity since the beginning and no one makes that as clear as Plato's philosophy on the warrior.

When Gideon and Purah go into the Midianite camp, Gideon discovers that Yahweh has filled the hearts of the enemy with fear through dreams and rumors of the valiant sword of Gideon. God has defeated enemy morale and Gideon did not know it. Gideon returns to Israel's camp and awakens the men. Gideon is humbled. He divides his men into three groups of one hundred and places them around the Midianite camp, leaving one area open for the Midianites to flee. In a bold display of 'smoke and mirrors', Gideon has his small group of 'dogs' blow their horns (shofars), burst their jars to expose their burning torches, and shout, "For Yahweh and for Gideon!"

In the midst of this loud and abrupt display, the Midianite men become so fearful they fight one another. In their effort to flee, they are completely disoriented by fear and trickery (wisdom). The men of Israel join in to take the land and some pursue to kill the kings that had warred against Israel.

Gideon fails to send his army of dogs home and the story takes a downward spiral as the grandeur of victory corrupts Gideon. Gideon has not understood the LORD who chose him to deliver Israel. Gideon, in one sense, becomes a type of king in Israel and his story collapses into violence. As a judge over Israel, Gideon becomes a failure because he did not go home, because he violates the behavior of a king or national leader, as written in Deuteronomy 17.

The Rules of War

Reading Deuteronomy 20

Introduction

The rules of war are written because Israel has failed to follow Yahweh in a trusting obedience that allows him to drive out the inhabitants with pestilence (e.g. Ex 23:28). Israel as a people is representative of humanity. They are the first fruits of God's harvest; their story is our story and their failures are our failures. The LORD cannot stop them from warring. This does not mean that Yahweh acquiesces and sanctions their militarization and murderous campaigns. Nor is Yahweh prohibited from participation in ways that instruct, circumvent, or function to determine the outcome. Likewise, the LORD can choose to depart and let men do what men do to one another.

War is a consuming practice that is in opposition to the will and desire of God. Wars are not creative acts that produce goods for human beings to enjoy. The LORD is so opposed to war that the scripture contains a challenge to Israel: the challenge to live without a military and to trust Yahweh. This blessing of the LORD's protection is dependent upon Israel's faithfulness to the LORD. Yahweh's desire is for a people, a nation that does not practice, or teach its children, to war (Isaiah 2:4, Micah 4:3).

The book of Deuteronomy begins with an enlightening note that claims entrance into the land could not take place until all the 'men of war' died. The message of this note is clear: warriors inhibit the way of God; they function in a way that is incompatible with the desire and hope of God. Warriors cannot live in the land of promise where the flourishing of life is expressed as milk and honey. War is not a way to peace, it is a way of life that can never bring the 'rest' that God desires for his people. War is a culture building, nationalist idol that requires a king (president). Joshua's wars did not bring 'rest' (Hebrews 4:8-11).

> *16 Just as soon as all the warriors*
> *had died off from among the people,*
> *(Deuteronomy 2:16 NRS)*

The warriors in this verse are those persons in the first chapter of Deuteronomy that were unwilling to go in and take the land in accordance with Yahweh's plan, a plan that resembled the exodus from Egypt. The exodus was an act of God and not a human military campaign. Israel was delivered from the power of Egypt by the LORD's hand (fear, pestilence, and ultimately loss of the firstborn). The challenge faced by these 'warriors' was to enter a land of giants and trust that Yahweh would route them out as the people moved forward into the land. When the men refused to go in (after the report of giants) Moses responded.

> *29 I said to you, "Have no dread or fear of them.*
> *30 The LORD your God, who goes before you,*
> *is the one who will fight for you, just as he did*
> *for you in Egypt before your very eyes,*
> *(Deuteronomy 1:29-30 NRS)*

Moses informs the people that their disobedience, their failure to go into the land, has resulted in the LORD's command that Moses lead them back into the wilderness. The males respond with strapping on their battle gear. This act defined them as warriors; it also revealed their lack of understanding: they were not to fight, but to let Yahweh fight for them as he did in Egypt (Ex 14:13-14; Deut 1:30). This group of 'warriors' will all die before Israel is allowed to return and enter the land. The lesson is clear; God did not want warriors; he wanted followers. The LORD wanted to be God and for Israel to be his people.[5]

When Israel enters the land after the death of the warriors, there is a disturbing difference: Israel will engage in warfare. The LORD is not going with them to fight for them as he did in Egypt. Yahweh cannot stop the people of the land from warring against Israel. This is problematic because it can result in the LORD acting as he did in Egypt when he was forced to kill the firstborn in order to gain the release of Israel.[6] Nonetheless, Yahweh

---

[5] The phrase 'I will be their God and they shall be my people' in various forms appears in the OT, it is referred to as the covenant formula. See: Rendtorf, Rolf. *The Covenant Formula: An Exegetical and Theological Investigation.* (Edinburgh: T & T Clark, 1998).

[6] In Egypt when Pharaoh told Moses he would kill him, it is to be understood that Pharaoh would also slaughter large numbers of Israel. The LORD has been patient in revealing God's self to Pharaoh and is concerned that Pharaoh understands Yahweh to be the one God, the creator. The LORD's plagues have each included mercy; God limited his coercive revelation of power. When Pharaoh chooses to take life, the LORD responds by demonstrating he is the Lord of life and so only the first-born die. There is no violence in their deaths their lives simply expire. God is not pleased with how this event

works to keep Israel from trusting in war. Yet, rather than engage humanity in a manner that leads to Yahweh directly taking life, the LORD must tolerate Israel's warring. The toleration of war by Yahweh is a problem, not a solution – a challenge, not absolute resignation to an inevitable reality.

The Herem (utter destruction)

The horror of the practice of Herem and its occurrences in the scripture is both terrifying and silencing. Nevertheless, I will attempt to write out my perspective on interpreting passages that seem to approve the practice of annihilating men, women, children and sometimes even the animals. First, lest we think of this barbarism as disconnected from the present era, let us remember the destruction caused by nuclear weapons. In contemporary practice, the killing of the masses is a justifiable act (e.g. drones and nuclear arsenals). It is an error to suppose there is any difference between the morality of moderns and the 'herem' practice of 'utter destruction' or 'annihilation' by the Israelites. The 'herem' suggests the only way to win a war is to kill the entire population of the people group that constitutes the 'enemy'. The thought being that their children will grow up to despise the killers of their people, and warring will continue.

The historical speeches of Moses in Deuteronomy can be read as an attempt to explain Israel's practice of annihilating human populations when taking their land, houses and cities. In Deuteronomy 1, the people Israel destroyed were offered payment to allow Israel to pass

---

reveals God's self and requires Israel to remember the great cost that purchased their release in the Passover ceremony.

through, but they refused. This refusal indicates that king Sihon's intent was to massacre Israel and take their stuff (likely their women also). He deferred on any form of payment and rejected peaceful passage through his land.

Israel must defend herself or be annihilated. Unleashing Israel to war under the banner of toleration, with the intent of taking the property of the people they conquer, led to the practice of annihilation. Further, the fear and dread of Israel would be built upon these initial encounters with the people of the land.

The practice of annihilation would have detrimental effects on those persons that participated in slaughtering innocents. This is likely to produce in Israelite society a growing rejection of the practice and a discontent with conquering. Yet the will to survive in the face of tyrannical kings willing to slaughter Israel, would result in raising the ire of the people and lean towards self-defense. The practice of slaughtering entire populations is not sustainable for developing a civilized society.

The assurance of Yahweh's will in their success does not contain any affirmation of intervention, nor is there any accompanying speech formula, (Thus says the LORD) to indicate direct involvement or approval from Yahweh. These early encounters from the historical section of Deuteronomy chapters one through four are records of Israel's failures and her role in decision-making for the unfolding of life in the land.

If you besiege a town for a long time, making war against it in order to take it, you must not destroy its trees by wielding an ax against them. Although you may take food from them, you must not cut them down. Are trees in the field human beings that they should come under siege from you? You may

destroy only the trees that you know do not produce food; you may cut them down for use in building siegeworks against the town that makes war with you, until it falls.
(Deuteronomy 20:19)

The final verse places the initial act of war on the town under siege. The real war, the problem, the difference, is ideological. The egalitarian rule of Yahweh in contrast to the erring superstitions of societies built upon domination and idolatry. A thinking person, like the people of Israel who have the Torah (law) read to them would be faced with choices on how to avoid war, rather than make trees more valuable than people. At the same time, wars end and life must continue.

A Story of Leyte Landing: War, Politics and the Generations

The future cannot be built upon memorials of war or alleged great men. The generations must be taught that most of these objects serve only as sad memories of a time when demagogues ruled with violence and humanity honored war. These mere images of stone and bronze have been used to deceive the masses. This story is about hope for a better world, the hope of a new generation.

Pictured are my three children and a mestiza (Filipino/American) girl named Gene. We met Gene in a squatter's area named Siren. These living children make better memories than McArthur and his group. Their lives speak of a history apart from the meaning of a war memorial. They are adults now and the era of U.S. liberation and domination is passing.

I am writing in 2016 and that generation of men that participated in World War II is left with only a few living representatives. I was living on the Island of Leyte in the Philippines when the forty-year anniversary and re-enactment of Macarthur's return was celebrated. In the biblical writings a generation is acknowledged in forty year time periods. The biblical idea is that the active influence of a generation upon the present begins somewhere around twenty years old, then fades and passes within around forty years.

In the book of Ecclesiastes 'Qohelet' (the author) states that a generation goes and a generation comes. Purposefully he begins his statement with death. Death is the sobering reality that causes us to question our life and the values we have lived by. I learned a valuable lesson from this dying group of old men. I also witnessed the ongoing drive of the living captured in the continual conflict of power and peace.

A Day to Remember

My friend, Levi Montes, worked at a local newspaper in the city of Tacloban. Tacloban is just a few kilometers from the Leyte Landing memorial. Levi was educated at FEAST (Far East Asian School of Theology) and maintained a house church in his upstairs apartment with his wife and growing number of children. James Balista was the President of Zion Bible College. I was holding weekly services at Leyte College. Levi acquired some press passes and the three of us were seated among local dignitaries on the speaker's platform. The speaker was Ferdinand Marcos, the dictator of the Philippines.

The day was a mixture of Marcos' politics and old soldiers (American, Japanese and Filipino) at the end of their lives, remembering dead friends, in the company of their former enemies. The day was marked by the excessive power of foreign forces on Philippine soil. War ships were in the bay, planes were overhead, explosive charges were blowing smoke and sand on the beach as a few men performed a mock battle. This display of power in memory of a past victory was overshadowed by the behavior of the veterans that had survived the battle, the war. I watched American men, their strength spent by time, their backs bowed and the presence of walking sticks had replaced guns. The Japanese men walked with the hobble that marks longevity, their faces reflected their years with tight skin and age marks. The Filipino men were few but present. Many of the Filipinos that fought alongside the American troops were not members of the Philippine military; U.S. forces recruited them to aid in reconnaissance and close combat. My father in-law was one of these men.

A lifetime had passed and the men that had been there forty years earlier, there on the shores of Leyte, locked in battle, killing each other, were there to remember, to say we survived. Then the release of emotions long held in silence began: an aging Japanese man and an aging American man embraced as tears flowed down their faces. After the re-enactment I scanned my eyes over the group of old veterans that had ventured out towards the beach I saw a number of men embracing each other, men that had once been enemies. I was twenty-eight years old. I saw them at a moment when age and the end of life brought them to their senses. The friends that were lost to the sins of the past had not been able to live full lives. Their lives were cut short by the warring aspirations of powerful leaders that can never acquire enough power. They had all been victims of history. Their war was not the last war, just another in the continuous succession of humanity's warring.

Marcos was in full-force, the consummate speaker and rhetorical master was warming up to a crowd-moving speech. His end as a dictator was in sight, but he would not be easily removed from his palace at Malacanang. I was seated with my pastor friends just a few feet behind the powerful dictator. I had seen the NPA rebel forces throughout Leyte and Samar. I wondered at his obstinate courage to stand out in an open-air platform facing a crowd of unknown people. His speech was primarily in the Visayan dialect Samarenyo (Waray Waray). The many foreign visitors were not able to capture the desperation of his last attempts to maintain power. My friends and I left the platform early, prior to the ending of Marcos' speech. We were all thinking that today might be the day a bullet would find the resilient dictator. The crowd pressed against the ropes and the area reserved for dignitaries and visitors was now public domain. Marcos would survive the day; his hold on power would end within a year's time.

The beauty of the picture at the head of this story is that these children, now grown, represent a generation of young people who do not view Marcos' reign, nor the imperial power of America, as honorable realities to be remembered. They are in a sense, children of war, touched by the reach of empire. My children and Gene are signs of hope. In their persons they unite separated peoples. Their view on the world is inclusive of difference and interested in peace over power. My son, Gregg, has gone on to found and lead Global Outreach Developments International, an organization that actively works to help the poor in six different nations through education, advocacy and empowerment.

When I look at the picture of this war memorial, I remember that U.S. forces had slaughtered as much as one sixth of the Philippine population during the Philippine American War (1898 to 1903). The possession of the Philippines was a successful effort to govern and control the resources of the small Asian nation. I remembered that the U.S. threatened to cripple Japan's economy with an oil embargo and this decision led to the Japanese attack upon Pearl Harbor.[7]

In the sixties, the Philippine American War was called 'America's first Viet Nam'. Before the U.S. was the Filipino savior, the U.S. was guilty of killing Filipino people without concern for their rights to live unmolested. It is difficult to establish a number for the civilians killed by U.S. forces. The lowest number for civilian deaths is 200,000. This low number is cushioned with the claim that cholera was responsible for many of the deaths. The Philippine historian E. San Juan, Jr, suggests a higher number of deaths (1,000,000) through military action that is equatable with genocidal warfare.[8]

The memorializing of war is merely a tool for the powers of a few to insure their wealth in the world. It is a myth that America liberated the Filipino.

---

[7] The many factors that led to the war between the U.S. and Japan are more complicated than the sole act of an oil embargo; nonetheless the oil embargo was a significant act of war upon the Japanese economy. See: Iriye, Akira. *The Origins of the Second World War in Asia and the Pacific*. (London, England: Longman Group, 1987) pg. 150.

[8] See: San Juan Jr., E. The Philippine Temptation: Dialectics of Philippines–U.S. Literary Relations. (Philadelphia PA. Temple University Press, 1996) pg. 2. That the number is higher is easily sustained by a perusal of historical documents containing communications between U.S. military officers revealing the general attitude of racism resonant in U.S. forces at the time. The estimated population of the Philippines by the Spanish was 6,000,000 persons. This would mean that U.S. forces killed one sixth of the Filipino population.

CHAPTER II

Heroes, Rebels and Zealots

Samson the Archetypal Strong Man

A man of exceptional strength is not an uncommon phenomenon in human history. Strength in a man can be as problematic as beauty for a woman: it tends to become an identity. Included in the story of Samson's feats of strength are his mother's story, his role as a deliverer, and the associative history of Israel. Samson is Israel's cultural product, a John Wayne, an action hero whose morals and deeds are left unquestioned in contemporary Christianity and within the text.

Samson's story in the book of Judges is identifiable as a genre of literature consistent with the time in which he lived. It was a time of heroes whose moral compass was less than admirable, whose cause was backed by a religious hope nearly lost, nearly abandoned. In an unsettled land of tribal violence legends were born through the exploits of men whose stories were marked by exaggerated feats of strength and courage. Their stories were the folk tales, the dime novels that captivated a people in need of heroic saviors.[9]

---

[9] Dime novels were initially printed in 1860 during the Wild West era of the United States. The inexpensive paperback books contained

In the canon of scripture these stories serve a variety of theological purposes. A study of the major female characters in Judges reveals a declension in the female voice.[10] When the female voice is silenced, the violence of genocide erupts. In this respect Judges is a book concerned with gender relations and the harm done when male machismo supplants gender equality. In the Samson story the voice of God is with Samson's mother and God's preference for her sits in contrast to her husband's failed leadership (Judges 13:2-23). She is called to live out a Nazarite vow and raise an exceptional child. Manoah's failure to submit to the role of his wife in relation to God and Samson results in Samson's character flaws. Although there is no king in Israel, the underlying social ill that plagues Israelite society is the ethics of male and female relationships.

After a forty-year period, the passing of a generation, the LORD chooses to provide Israel with another judge, another deliverer (Samson). Yet Samson's story is one of failure, particularly the failures of Samson and his father. In a sense, Israel is like Samson.

Israel's greatest enemies are not Philistines, but her failure to live as God's people. When Israel fails to live according to her calling, then God delivers Israel over to the power of the Philistines. The Philistines epitomize Israel's

---

a genre of story built upon extrapolation of stories about violent or marginal people as anti-heroes. Samson is an anti-hero. He is not an exemplar for faith, behavior, morals or male / female relationships.

[10] See: Garner, Mike *Interpretive Adventures; Subversive Readings in a Missional School*, (West Conshoshocken, PA: Infinity Publishing, 2015) Chapter IV.

perennial enemy: an immoral society, a people who imagine multiple gods, cosmic spirits of the universe. It is apparent that the people of Israel are a distinct people only when they live in covenant with the LORD. As a people, they share biological relatedness with numerous other groups in the land. Their tribal identities are more situational (political) than biological.

Although the land is given rest, it is apparent the people are not entering the rest. The land's abundance is God's gift and not Israel's righteousness. God and land are at rest, but the people are without a king; there is no order in the land. Without God there is no order in society. Nonetheless, in the book of Judges God's goodness rains upon a troubled land where people are populating and the ground is flourishing.

The story of Samson begins with his mother. The narrator emphasizes her barrenness. The heavenly messenger charges her to live according to the Nazarite vow (c.f. Judg 13.2-5 and Num 6). There is no reason to limit her living as a Nazarite to end after Samson's birth. Living according to the Nazarite vow serves as a sign of God's efforts to form the child into a person dedicated to the LORD. That Samson's mother participates in the vow with Samson is indicative of God's intended role for her as the major influence in Samson's life. This is also made clear because the messenger of the LORD appears to and prefers to speak with her.

The messenger of the LORD appears to Manoah's nameless wife. Her namelessness is indicative of an incomplete identity, of a suppressed minority, the female gender. In the story the LORD identifies with the nameless female, calls her to a Nazarite life, blesses her with a child, and requires her to be the major influence in the life of Samson. Manoah does not examine his life to uncover why he is an unacceptable role model for the promised child. Rather, he seeks to control the divine events through ritual and spoils his son.

> *But Samson said to his father,*
> *"Get her for me, because she pleases me."*
> *(Judges 14:3 NRS)*

Manoah's nameless wife refers to the angel of the Lord as a man. When Manoah prays for an audience with the messenger of the Lord, he appears a second time to Manoah's wife. She brings Manoah to the 'man'. The messenger limits Manoah's participation in the rearing of Samson. Manoah is to enable his wife to fulfill all the words spoken to her. The messenger of the Lord will not accept Manoah's hospitality. Manoah is not like Abraham. Manoah is only told to support his wife in her efforts to live as the messenger has commanded. Although God responds to Manoah's prayer to be brought into the appearances of the messenger, he must 'walk behind' his wife for the meeting.

> *Manoah got up and followed his wife,*
> *and came to the man and said to him,*
> *"Are you the man who spoke to this woman?"*
> *And he said, "I am."*
> *Then Manoah said, "Now when your words come true,*
> *what is to be the boy's rule of life;*
> *what is he to do?"*
> *The angel of the LORD said to Manoah,*
> *"Let the woman give heed to all that I said to her.*
> *(Judges 13:11-13 NRS)*

She is nameless throughout the narrative and in this manner is like God, who refuses to be named or be identified by a name at Manoah's request. Manoah is not like Moses. God's encounter with Manoah is marked by the tension of Manoah's inability to view his wife as an equal. He insists on a sacrifice since the messenger refuses his hospitality. Manoah is convinced only after the messenger vanishes upward with the flames. Manoah's sacrificial exercise is aimed at gaining some control of the events that have touched his wife's life. The stinging intent of the writer seems to be that even as your wife is not named - only a woman in your story- so god is only a nameless apparition who disappears in the light of some flames. Manoah's priestly effort to control his wife's religious experience and divine encounter is marked as a failure when she corrects his erring comments after the messenger disappears. Manoah's wife believes the message, the words, whereas Manoah believes his sight and does not abide by or hear the words of the messenger.

Manoah attempts to align his experience with the Israelites at the mountain. He fears death is near because they have spoken with God. She (Manoah's wife) corrects the erring theology of her husband and receives the spoken word.[11]

> *And Manoah said unto his wife, We shall surely die,*
> *because we have seen God.*
> *But his wife said unto him, If the LORD*
> *were pleased to kill us,*

---

[11] This is a phenomenal moment, it reflects Deuteronomy 5 when Israel refused the voice of God and Moses was required to write laws, ordinances and statutes. God desired to speak with Israel but they feared because their hearts were not right. Manoah's wife displays a heart like Moses'.

> *he would not have received a burnt offering and a meat offering at our hands,*
> *neither would he have shewed us all these things,*
> *nor would as at this time have told us such things as these.*
> *(Judges 13:22-23 KJV)*

The Exodus story begins with women: a mother, a sister, and some brave midwives. In Samuel, the story of Israel's becoming a nation-state begins with a woman (Hannah). Hannah's influence in the life of Samuel surpasses that of her arrogant wealthy husband and of Eli the erring priest and failed father. So it is in the Samson story, it begins with a promise, a woman, and hope. In Judges, God is found in the weak, the humble, in acts of mercy and not in the surface story of powers that act with violence.

Finding God in a story like Samson's requires acknowledging the absence of God and the radical monotheism of the author(s) who allow for grace in the terror of violence and war. The popular propaganda of Israel's wealthy caused the poor to look to heroes for explaining her survival. The scribal community that produced the scripture sought to uncover the root cause of Israel's problems. First, of course, is keeping the Torah, the covenant with God. Second was to uncover the perennial problems of violence and gender relations, of the failing pietism of ritual practice and symbolic nationalism. Further, these wise men wrote in a manner that subverts the official story and challenges concepts of inevitability in relation to violence.

Samson is the archetypal strong man; he is an esthetic personality, a creature of vanity and desire. As a human being, he is a shallow display of arrogance, lust, and vengeance. Samson is an unethical character; he is not a religious person, he violates his Nazarite status without remorse. Samson cannot even discern the presence of the Lord. For Samson, God's presence is merely the adrenaline of human strength.

> *But he did not know that the LORD had left him.*
> *(Judges 16:20 NRS)*

Samson's first words reveal a man who sees, desires, and demands (Judges 14:2,3). Samson's first display of strength is not witnessed by anyone. Men do not kill lions with their bare hands: unless the lion is sick and dying, or wounded in a pit. In Samson's world, the carcasses of dead animals produce bees (spontaneously). The imagery of the Lion and the honey, in contrast with the imagery of the jawbone and the water, is telling (this will be explored later in this chapter).

Samson is on the way to Timnah to take a wife from the Philistines when he turns aside to see the carcass of the dead lion. He scoops some honey into his hand and shares it with his mother and father. He does not tell them the story of how the lion died. Perhaps his exaggerated displays of strength would not have impressed his parents.

The dynamic between Samson and his wife is the same as it will be with Delilah. The scene is nearly repetitive in the sense that both women betray Samson when their tribal group is in conflict with Samson. The first group seeks to solve the riddle in order to win a wager. The second group seeks to uncover the secret of Samson's strength in order to defeat him, torture him, mock him, make him a public spectacle and invalidate the myth of his heroic status.

In the first scene, Samson justifies his murder of Philistine men because they had 'ploughed with his heifer': threatened to murder her family. Samson makes good on the wager but does so through an act of vengeance upon innocent persons. He is also aware of a degree of guilt.

> *"This time, when I do mischief to the Philistines,
> I will be without blame."*
> *(Judges 15:3 NRS)*

When Samson returns to see his wife, she has been given to another, to Samson's best man. In true heroic fashion, the storyteller claims the great fire set by Samson was accomplished through the capture of 300 foxes! After a brief description of a battle where Samson strikes the enemy hip and thigh (an allusion to Jacob's nighttime encounter), he spends the night in the cleft of a rock (an allusion to Moses' experience).[12] However, Samson offers no prayers, seeks only vengeance and God never appears to him.

The Philistines come out in force against the Israelite group. This act causes Samson's own tribal group to seek to bind and deliver him over to the Philistines. He agrees only to break the bonds and ignite a battle. Samson is accredited with killing a thousand men.[13] The remarkable number is even more absurd when we consider that Samson struck them with the fresh jawbone of an ass. In a moment of severe thirst, after speaking in anger to

---

[12] The cleft is name Etam and is possibly the name of an animal a beast.

[13] David has killed his ten thousands is a chant sung by Israel's maidens when David has returned from slaying Goliath; David is exalted beyond his exploits.

God, Samson sucks the (juice) marrow from the bone as though it was water and so he is revived.[14]

In the mind of the reader, the storyteller has provided three distinct images: the lion, the foxes and the jawbone of an ass. Samson had the opportunity to provide sweetness in the world with the strength of a lion but he shared his strength (the honey from the lion's carcass) only with his mother and father. Samson had the opportunity to be as cunning as a fox but he violated the rules of war and caused a wildfire that destroyed both grape vines and olive groves.[15] Samson did not have the education to know that Moses was prohibited from entering the land because he struck the rock after being told to speak to it. Samson does not practice diplomacy or efforts at peacemaking. Samson incites violence. Samson-like Ishmael is a wild ass of a man. He is on no one's side. He sucks the marrow from the ass's jawbone; there is no speech, only desire and instinct.

Samson's demand for God to provide him some sustenance reflects his spoiled character. His words do not qualify as a prayer; rather, they reflect Samson's desire for immediate physical recovery. Samson claims the battle was a great deliverance and addresses himself as a servant, but his words lack any humility and he does not address God with any appellative.

---

[14] A divine intervention on the scale of duplicating a miracle similar to Moses is inconsistent with the Samson narrative. I do not think we are to understand that a spring of water was miraculously brought forth at Lehi. Rashi the Jewish commentator understands Judges 15:19 to read that Samson drank water through a tooth socket in the jawbone of an ass.

[15] See Deuteronomy 20:19,20.

> *¹⁸ And he was very thirsty, and he called on the*
> *LORD and said,*
> *"Thou hast granted this great deliverance*
> *by the hand of thy servant;*
> *and shall I now die of thirst, and*
> *fall into the hands of the uncircumcised?"*
> *(Judges 15:18 RSV)*

So, Samson's pretense at receiving divine aid by drinking water from the jawbone of an ass after striking the Philistines is comical. How much water can you get from the hollow of an ass' jawbone? Samson does not know his people's history, their God, or their law.

After Samson's claim to have slain a thousand men, he speaks to God. When the messenger of the LORD spoke to his mother, the messenger used the particle of entreaty 'na' – meaning, 'pray' or 'beg' – to require that she take on the Nazarite vow. Samson calls upon God and demands water. Samson lives like an animal and derives life from carcasses and bones. Samson is not a wise man, not a prophet, not a peacemaker. Samson is a bully, a man who consorts with prostitutes. The book of Judges exposes the absurdity of viewing a man like Samson as a hero (but this is what people do).

> *But God clave an hollow place that was in the jaw,*
> *and there came water thereout;*
> *and when he had drunk, his spirit*
> *came again, and he revived:*
> *wherefore he called the name thereof Enhakkore,*
> *which is in Lehi unto this day.*
> *(Judges 15:19 KJV)*

The etiologies for the place names of Ramath-lehi and Enhakkore are two separate pieces that identify the same location. Samson cast away the jawbone and named the place Ramath-lehi. He then picked up the jawbone and drank from the tooth socket and named it Enhakkore (supposedly the name of a spring). Names and place names are difficult to establish meaning for, based upon identifying possible root words, although Ramath-lehi in the ears of a Hebrew speaking person is easily heard as maggots of an ass's jawbone.

Samson is a man in rebellion. His Nazarite vow has not made him a devout man, a follower of the LORD. His water miracle is comical, his naming ironic, Samson is a man to be pitied, a man who has wasted his gift of strength. The book of Judges appeals to the reader to escape the popular love for, and pursuit of, heroes. The only Judge of any moral character is Deborah (Judges 4-5) and her non-violent followers.[16]

Samson, the philandering brute, stops in Gaza to sleep with a prostitute and awakes in the middle of the night to depart carrying off the city gates on his shoulders. His acts of strength and behavior are a mockery to all that represents a moral life of wisdom.

Samson's name is related to the Hebrew word for sun. The writer of Genesis avoids using the word 'shemesh' when speaking of the bigger light, in order to avoid any

---

[16] It is arguable that Deborah is non-violent first because her calling of Barak to go and fight seems to be an intentional effort to entrap him in his pursuit for glory and diminish his stature as a warrior. Further Deborah functions as an oracular prophetess whose lack of power is designated by the Palm tree she sits under.

idea that God created other gods. The naming of Samson (Shimshon) by his mother is curious. On the one hand, she names her son while she remains nameless. On the other hand, the naming of Samson occurs after Manoah has attempted to be the primary recipient of the divine encounter through his priestly activities. Perhaps the naming of Samson is because his mother knows that she will not be able to influence him in a life of devotion to the Lord. How Samson will shine is left up to his own choosing.

The legend of Samson's strength is set in contrast to the power of Delilah, the amorous woman. The seduction of Samson's will takes place in the bedchamber of a powerfully sensuous woman. Samson's encounter with the prostitute at Gaza requires a brief rest, then he walked off with the gates of the city. This time Samson's sexual parlay with Delilah will drain him of his will and ultimately his strength. Samson's strength is portrayed in the book of Judges as both feats of physical power and sexual virility.

It is apparent that Samson's sexual marathon with Delilah is a game set against the backdrop of betrayal. His wife and his countrymen have previously betrayed Samson; there is no reason for him to consider Delilah's questioning as innocent curiosity. Rather, her questioning is in contrast to the former event with his wife over the solution to his riddle.

In the final scene, Samson is asleep with his head lying on the knees of Delilah. She has drained Samson's sexual energy and in effect also broken his will. Samson has revealed his belief regarding the source of his extraordinary strength. His Nazarite status has been symbolic only and lacked evidence of a dedicated life to the LORD. Samson exemplifies a non-religious person given to superstition. The hair on his head is not the source of his strength. Delilah is intelligent enough to know that the combined exertion of sexual energy and the broken will of Samson is enough to weaken him so that he can be defeated. She announces his defeat prior to their last sexual romp, puts him to sleep on her knees and has men in wait ready to cut off his hair. Delilah knows Samson's strength lies in his heart, his will.

*And when Delilah saw that he had told her all his heart,
she sent and called for the lords of the Philistines, saying,
Come up this once, for he hath shewed me all his heart.
Then the lords of the Philistines came up unto her,
and brought money in their hand.
(Judges 16:18 KJV)*

Part of the lesson in the book of Judges, and in particular in the story of Samson, is that strength and virility are gifts of God. Even adrenaline is a gift of God and these physical gifts are part of the richness of life. The spirit of God in the Samson story is not equatable with the presence of the Holy Spirit indwelling a human being, but the blessing of life that comes from God. The monotheism of the writer(s) allowed for these very human blessings to be indicative of God's goodness to a human being. How a person uses these gifts lies within their will, their heart.

Samson is bound, tortured and mocked. While in prison, his hair (his will) begins to grow. Samson, bound between two pillars, is an object of mockery.[17] Samson's final act of strength is an act of suicidal vengeance, not a model for blessing. However, prior to his collapsing the

---

[17] In spite of her strength Israel is dying a self-induced death, suffering blindness and mockery, chained between the pillars of Dagon.

temple of Dagon, Samson prayed for God to bless him with strength, one more time. His reason was because he sought vengeance for the loss of his two eyes.

The deliverance Samson offered to Israel is found in the exposure of male machismo. Israel needs delivered from philandering with Philistine society. The Philistines represent Israel's perennial enemy as an immoral society. The Samson story ends with a picture of Israel: she is like Samson, blessed with strength and virility, but she has become blind and mocked. Israel is an esthetic people lacking ethical or spiritual development. The story of Samson challenges the people of Israel to choose to follow the LORD. Manoah's failure to follow his nameless wife is Israel's challenge to recognize that the LORD speaks to women. Israel is challenged to establish a just society where women can be Nazarites, speak with God, and priests give up their rituals to build a just society where gender relations are not marked by abuse but health and love.

The story of the anti-hero Samson ends in death and the collapse of Dagon's temple. Israel's deliverer faces the same end as her enemies. It is a meaningful picture, as an archetype, the strong man Samson represents Israel's concept of deliverance and ideas of strength. His life reflects Israel's efforts to take the land. The lesson of his life is that Israel will perish with her enemies if she does not change. The Samson story is written to challenge Israel to consider how she is to live in the land with other peoples. How is Israel to defeat her enemies? Who are her enemies? These questions are literary motifs; e.g. Samson is his own enemy. Samson's way is not God's way. The book of Judges teaches that violence escalates and is self-destructive.

The challenge of the book of Judges is for Israel to learn to live at peace as male and female, as equals, with mutual respect, to raise their children together, to be moral, faithful to the Lord who longs to provide the land for them as an inheritance. Israel is challenged to embrace the people of the land and defeat them by winning them over, by being the people of God. As scripture, the book of Judges exposes universal truths about the human struggle. Judges lays the problem of war and violence on males who dominate society, religion, and women.

Korah's Rebellion a Conflict, Contrasting Spirit, Word and Law

Introduction

I will be practicing a final form reading of the Korah story. Narrative continuity, based upon the role of the surrounding stories and established characters, will be the guiding lens for many (not all) of my theological claims. I am aware of form and redaction criticism in relation to the book of Numbers; however, this story can be read without identifying any editorial work based upon the popular JEDP consensus. It is my view of scripture that the stories of Israel were primarily written for our instruction and are not subject to the modern literalist effort to produce a factual history without imaginative elements.

The value of any interpretive effort is its power to change the life of another, to draw them closer to God. It is my pursuit to bring God closer to the reader via the scripture and within the constructs of a responsible hermeneutic.

Israel's scribes wrote their spiritual and intellectual revelations through the use of their history. At times the fine line between history and invention are difficult if not impossible to discern. At other times the text offers literary clues through the use of mythic characters. Occasionally the author leaves obvious contradictory statements within the text, in order for the reader to revisit previously read passages and reconsider the meaning of the text in light of competing claims.

I will begin by appealing to two passages from Numbers in order to establish the use of myth and of contradiction as applicable to the Korah story. First, Numbers 13:33 references the children of Anak, who were descendants of the Nephilim (or giants).[18] The introduction of myth as congruent with the literary style or genre(s) of the book of numbers is to alert the reader to the playfulness of the writers and their use of myth. The claim of the spies to have seen the sons of Anak is neither disputed nor denied; there is no textual deconstruction to expose myth. It sits as an uneasy element in the text and displays the use of myth as a normative part of storytelling. Second, Numbers 26:11 clearly states that the children of Korah did not die, contrary to the story in Numbers 16.

> *The descendants of Eliab: Nemuel, Dathan, and Abiram. These are the same Dathan and Abiram, chosen from the congregation, who rebelled against Moses and Aaron in the company of Korah, when they rebelled against the Lord,*

---

[18] The Nephilim appear first in the proto-historical narratives of Genesis 1-11. These mythopoeic stories present theological teaching on universal realities about the human condition. Genesis 1-11 also represents responses to myths in the ancient near eastern world that were present at the time of the writing of Genesis 1-11.

and the earth opened its mouth and swallowed them up along with Korah, when that company died, when the fire devoured two hundred fifty men; and they became a warning. Notwithstanding, the sons of Korah did not die.
(Numbers 26: 9-11)

The reduction of the text to surface instruction on Moses' superiority, resistance to the democratization of the priesthood, and the role of the Levites, fails to address the philosophical and theological efforts of Moses and Israel's scribes. We are not reading a text that communicates law as absolute, but as instructive. Torah is teaching and law is to be studied, not merely enforced. The approach to law as immovable makes law and violence inseparable.[19] Portrayals of divine violence are used to abolish the immovable nature of law when read as absolute. These portrayals are then subject to the literary inventions of Israel's storytellers that include the use of myth and contradiction. They are writing theology and learning about the God whose self-revelation is progressive, instructive and life-giving. Their history is the backdrop of their search for God.

---

[19] I think this is why the death penalty refrain in the OT exists. It teaches us that law is violent and the only way law can end human failing is to kill everyone. The end of law is truly death in the sense that we justify law to the point that 'kherem' is justifiable. In the modern world this is accomplished through the indiscriminate killing of bombs and the sinful immoral horror of nuclear weapons. War is someone's claim to legal rights e.g. 'self interest' it is also madness, a collective insanity built on the idolatry of nationalism.

Narrative Setting and Continuity

Moses is the major character throughout Exodus, Leviticus, Numbers and Deuteronomy. His journey has been long and his life filled with changes. Moses is a man (although he was 'god' to Pharaoh – Exodus 7:1). He is not a faultless representation of God (YHWH); he is learning to follow, learning to find God through his life, through revelation, and is subject to numerous failings. In this sense, Moses learns along the way and is granted some grace. After all, Moses lived prior to the consummate revelation of God in Jesus.

Moses learned that violence does not work when he murdered an Egyptian only to be reviled by the persons he intended to help. The temptation to power sustained by violence is Moses' personal revelation in relation to humanity and to God. The fire of God does not consume the bush where he speaks with Moses. Moses learns that it is so safe in God's presence he can remove his shoes in the middle of the wilderness. He enters into the hospitality of God. The scene awaits its consummate fulfillment in the moment when Jesus washes Peter's feet.

Moses' sister Miriam saved his life, watching over his precarious but carefully placed basket along the Nile. Was it Miriam's boldness in the presence of Pharaoh's daughter that opened the way for Moses to live and become an Egyptian? Moses' sister is a prophetess; she also struggles with the exceptional status of Moses in relation to God. When Moses was alone and needed a partner, God spoke to Aaron who ventured into the wilderness to find his younger brother. Aaron lacks the inner fortitude to withstand the voice of the people. The cause of his weakness is similar to that of all human beings, the inability to stand alone in the face of the crowd: Moses' history included a family who experienced God in relation to Moses' life (at least this is all we see in the history).

Moses' role as a chosen soul conflicts with the humility that marks his life as an old man. At the same time, Moses' perennial struggle is the temptation to power marked by violence rather than speech. This reality is so important that it becomes Moses' downfall and he will not be allowed to enter the land of promise. Moses, the man who spoke with God face to face, must die like all men.

Moses' wife is not interested in his efforts to become a socio-political religious leader of slaves. He has unresolved problems with Zipporah and sends her home only to have Jethro bring her and his sons back. Moses is not merely a social visionary; he is a man of faith whose pursuit of God is greeted with a challenge that mixes the man with the God. Moses longs that this would be so for all people – that all people would learn to speak for God, to speak the words of God. In this sense, Moses is a victim of history because the Spirit is not yet given freely to all. His teaching is exhibited in his life as one who would be a faithful servant in the house of God.

As an archetypal prophet, Moses' life of faith is rendered in stories of grand encounters with the divine. Whether alone, with family, in the company of many, or of demagogues, Moses brings God into the world even as God educates Moses over the course of his life. He learned that the violence indigenous to humanity would not be overcome until God gave freely of himself to all humanity. So, he wrote law to limit the damage of humanity's inherent violence. Moses established religious symbols, ceremonies, and memories to tame human arrogance and provide an institution that would preserve the revelation of God in history.

The generation that died over the course of the wilderness wanderings is identified in particular as the men of war (Joshua 5:1-6). They fought with God and they fought with Moses; they fought king Sihon and king Og. The qualifying reason for their exclusion from the land and their death as wandering condemned men is that they had no imagination for a world without the violence of war.

The Violence of Law or the Spirit of Reasoned Speech

The appearance of younger men in mass accompanying an old man is always a signal of impending violence. Younger men thoughtlessly flock to an older man with power and reputation. In mass, they become a crowd and lack the one attribute that separated Moses from everyone: Moses would stand alone with his faith in goodness, in God. When these younger men (in relation to Korah) who have distinguished themselves as 'men of renown' - a phrase used only Numbers 16:2 and Genesis 6:4 - stand with Korah, they in effect stand in the violence and abuse that marked the sons of god, the Nephilim. The literary use of this phrase purposefully reveals the ambition of these men as void of any altruistic desire; rather, they are seeking their own exaltation in order to rule over the people.

Noah's flood is the eruption of the chaotic waters in response to the violence that filled the earth. The use of phrases that link the book of Numbers and the Korah story to Genesis chapter six alert the reader to two realities. One is that violence is the intention of Korah and his company. The other is that the creation will respond to their intended violence. The story in

Numbers 16 reports these events in a narrative with the speech of God and Moses pointing to the monotheistic understanding of the writers. The power behind creation is God's, the outcome God's intent.

Moses understands the impending use of violence that is at the root of their rebellion; they intend a violent removal of Moses from power; they intend to kill Moses. Moses throws himself face down on the ground, a defenseless man who refuses to contend with their show of ready violence. The text places Moses face down and does not say he rose to speak. To kill Moses when he is in a position of surrender would be an act of murder and lack the contest Korah needs. There is nothing courageous or honorable in killing an old man. Moses understands nonviolent resistance.

> *When Moses heard it, he fell on his face. Then he said to Korah and all his company, "In the morning the Lord will make known who is his, and who is holy, and who will be allowed to approach him; the one whom he will choose he will allow to approach him.*
> *(Numbers 16:4-5)*

Moses' prayer includes his statement of innocence; he has not 'taken' anything from anyone for his personal gain. Moses' prayer affirms his understanding of Korah and his group, their democratization of holiness is a farce, they intend to use religion as a tool for demagoguery and personal gain. Moses' speech in Numbers 17: 5-16 is spoken by Moses while he is lying on the ground in a defenseless posture of humility.

> *15 And Moses was very wroth, and said unto the LORD,*
> *Respect not thou their offering: I have not*
> *taken one ass from them, neither have I hurt one of them.*
> *(Numbers 16:15 KJV)*

Moses appealed to the leaders of the revolt and gave them opportunity to consider their actions. He gave them an evening to prepare an offering (based upon Moses' prayer it is likely that they acquired the offering by taking it from weaker persons). Moses notes their pretense to holiness and provides a ceremonial moment for determining who is holy. Moses also appeals to Dathan and Abiram who set the scene as a contest for violence. They claim Moses intends to blind them (cut out their eyes) and is little more than a failed Pharaoh. The forces of Korah, his company, pursue a violent change of power. The ceremony gives them opportunity to display their great dedication to the burgeoning nationalism that needs to assimilate the religion of Israel in order to win the hearts of all the people.

Moses speaks from a position of surrender, while his opposition ends speech (word) with impending violence. Korah prefers the display of ceremony. Dathan and Abiram reject speech (diplomacy) for accusations of intended violence, a display of mistrust in order to promote an act of justified violence based upon claims of Moses' failure to deliver promises of land with milk and honey (i.e. a land flourishing with life where animals populate and bees produce honey).

It is a moment of crisis, of an impending and certain eruption of violence. Moses fears that this moment will end in the destruction of all that God has done to produce a people. He fears they will be consumed. Moses intercedes and asks God to deliver the people from the influence (the sin) of the one man (Korah).

> [26] *And he spake unto the congregation, saying,
> Depart, I pray you, from the tents of these wicked men,
> and touch nothing of theirs,
> lest ye be consumed in all their sins.*
> *(Numbers 16:26 KJV)*

Violence is self-destructive. Violence calls forth the powers of creation to erupt and swallow up the disharmonious uncreative existence of Korah's rebellion. Creation is life; violence is death. Moses understands that these men have brought upon themselves the powers of death. The mouth of the earth swallows up Korah. The two hundred and fifty are lost to their own fire offering in the tumult caused by the eruption of the earth that swallowed Korah. The violence of the people against the two hundred and fifty was part of the chaos of the moment, and the people fear a similar fate as Korah.

Moses' speech asks God to create, not to kill but to create an end to the lives of those that would destroy all the people in order to gain power. Isn't this the result of violence, the accumulation of destructive power until all life is threatened? God answers Moses' prayer; it is in one sense a sign act. The earth speaks, opens her mouth and returns violent men (who refuse speech) to the ground. Into Sheol, they fall alive and the earth closes. They return to the adamah (ground) from which humanity was created. They enter Sheol alive but they no longer share in life under the sun. Creation has spoken, violence is intolerable, and it was God who created the speech.

I understand that God's response (opening the mouth of the earth to swallow Moses' opposition) can be thought of as an act of redemptive or virtuous violence; the text resists this through use of the word 'bara' (create).

The story invites humanity to imagine a world where nonviolence prevails, where creation works in concert with nonviolent persons – a world where dialogue and the humility of helplessness, of nonviolent response, overcomes the men of renown.

In this case, we are reading stories of God's progressive revelation. In this particular story, the life of those swallowed up returns to the adamah (Sheol). Can they be restored or is the chasm unbreachable?

> *O that you would hide me in Sheol,*
> *that you would conceal me until your wrath is past,*
> *that you would appoint me a set time, and remember me*
> Job 14:13

Are these moments of divine violence difficult for God? Of course, the text portrays God as angry and attributes to God human understanding of his response. This portrayal of God as angry is inconsistent with the revelation of God on the cross praying for the forgiveness of those who murder him. There is an effort in scripture to understand these moments as the creation's response to the immoral and unethical actions of humanity. I think we also see reflected in this story the idea of an ecological hot zone. I mean that the presence of God is so near, so manifested as to cause creation to reject persons resistant God.

An Ecological Hot Zone

I will provide more thought on the concept of an ecological hot zone and God's manifest presence. First, it is imperative that my reader grasps the theological understanding of humanity's ethical and moral connection with the ground (the creation). In the creation story, Adam and Eve's choice to reach for the fruit (beyond the underlying structures of reality) results in a change in creation. The world becomes hostile to life, the ground is cursed and thorns appear on the plant life. This is the first place in the canon where the ethical and moral behavior of humanity affects the ground.

One of the more popular expressions of this theological theme is II Chronicles 7:14.

If my people who are called by my name humble themselves,
pray, seek my face, and turn from their wicked ways,
then I will hear from heaven,
and will forgive their sin and heal their land.

The book of Hosea is rich with the theological theme that humanity's moral behavior affects the ground.

There is no faithfulness or loyalty,
and no knowledge of God in the land.
Swearing, lying, and murder,
and stealing and adultery break out;
bloodshed follows bloodshed.
Therefore the land mourns,
and all who live in it languish;
together with the wild animals
and the birds of the air,
even the fish of the sea are perishing.

Paul affirms this theology in Romans 8:19-20.

For the creation waits with eager longing
for the revealing of the children of God;
for the creation was subjected to futility,
not of its own will but by the will of the one
who subjected it, in hope that the creation itself will
be set free from its bondage to decay and will obtain
the freedom of the glory of the children of God

It is apparent that the scripture presents a metaphysical connection of humanity and creation. How is God involved in this reality? It is the revelation of God in scripture that separates God from the created order.[20] Israel's monotheism does not deify the cosmos in any sense. So, humanity is connected to the cosmos inasmuch as when humanity fails to image God, to be like Jesus, then an uncreative power is released that harms the world. It seems that God who is merciful and redemptive makes room for a reality that is inconsistent with his person and presence. That reality is the instructive presence of death brought into the world as God's design and humanity's freedom to create reality. As the scriptural revelation unfolds, in the end, God destroys death as the final enemy (1 Cor 15:26)

Humanity then has the potential to bring God into the world by living morally ethical lives rooted in faith. In what sense is God absent from the uncreative reality of human 'sin'? I will utilize the words 'presence' and 'essence' to explain the reality of God's manifestation in contrast to the reality of God's absence in 'sin' and 'un-creation'. How is God present everywhere yet absent, or at the least refusing to participate in reality? Chapter III in this section is on Hosea and the absence of God. I will explore aspects of God's absence in the world and propose a way of understanding God's manifest presence in contrast to God's (if you will) absence.

---

[20] Exodus 34: 5-8 is God's self –revelation. Who God is in contrast to how God is viewed through the created order is evident in the division of the poetic piece (God Speech) at the end of line b of verse 7. The first half of the poem is God's self-description. The second half is how God is viewed through the creation's (humanity's) experience.

It is my view of scripture's revelation of God that God is a being. For this reason, theology is always ontological. The old argument that being precedes essence is not my concern. I will speak of God's essence as 'Spirit' and of God's presence (being) as the movement (manifestation) of God (who is Spirit). God's manifest presence as Spirit is distinguished from the silence, the hiddenness, of God's essence as Spirit.

With this defining of language, it can be said that God's essence is everywhere, but the manifestation of God's being (presence) is made known by movement, by the capability of human consciousness to recognize the presence of God. However, human beings need not be present for God to be manifest, e.g. as the creation event begins the Spirit of God 'moves' over the waters.

Conclusion

The rebellion of Korah occurs at a moment when God is near (present). Moses has brought God into the world through his act of non-violent resistance accompanied with a moral life and prayerful speech. God is also present because Israel as a people comprises a covenant role in God's salvific and redemptive activity. God's self-revelation is threatened by the actions of Korah and his band of violent murderers.

Violence is a plague upon humanity. Once released, it escalates like a fire ignited in oil. The response of the people on the following day is remarkable, if the entire event is marked with the dramatic power of divine intervention it claims. Yet this callous response is consistent with the wilderness generation. Their hardness of heart is unexplainable. In spite of their witness to the divine power, they have missed the divine mercy; the power was blinking. I suspect the plague was the release of violence in the congregation as they bickered over how to contend with Moses and his God. Has the maddening crowd erupted into killing one another? We are not told. The plague and the number of dead is a comment upon the loss of life due to the arousal of violence initiated by the desire for power in a few.

> *And when the congregation had assembled against them, Moses and Aaron turned toward the tent of meeting; the cloud had covered it and the glory of the LORD appeared. Then Moses and Aaron came to the front of the tent of meeting, and the LORD spoke to Moses, saying, "Get away from this congregation, so that I may consume them in a moment." And they fell on their faces. Moses said to Aaron, "Take your censer, put fire on it from the altar and lay incense on it, and carry it quickly to the congregation and make atonement for them. For wrath has gone out from the LORD; the plague has begun." So Aaron took it as Moses had ordered, and ran into the middle of the assembly, where the plague had already begun among the people. He put on the incense, and made atonement for the people. He stood between the dead and the living; and the plague was stopped. Those who died by the plague were fourteen thousand seven hundred, besides those who died in the affair of Korah.*
> *(Numbers 16:42-49)*

Aaron's ceremony in the midst of the plagued congregation testifies to their condition; symbolic ceremony is more powerful for them than speech. They need their religion. Religion is not the cause of violence but is able to restrain violence. Religion can be co-opted by the violent, but religion resists violence. Co-opted religion is for those who do not know how to speak peace. Good religion is for those who have heard the call of God to a Kingdom without violence.

Horror, Zealotry, and Phinehas

Preparation for Reading Numbers 25:1-18

It is apparent the OT contains traditions that attribute to God Israel's own desire for vengeance and security through acts of intolerable violence.[21] These traditions are more a reflection of the ideology of the times than a testimonial experience penned by Moses. Likewise, Moses' commands are often subjected to the needs of the story for justification of Israel's actions. In some cases (as with the Phinehas story) the story itself deconstructs the statement attributed to Moses (25:1-5).

Israel viewed the use of violence as an inevitable facet of existence. This is so in part because the natural world works violently against life with all sorts of disease and calamity. In contradistinction to this view are the OT's numerous examples of God calling Israel to nonviolence. The resulting tension is between the human voice, which tries to make God culpable for all of reality (violence), and God's refusal to accept culpability for humanity's violent acts. The hostility of the world present in natural catastrophe, disease, deformity, and the brevity of life contributes to the human need to make God culpable.

The presence of violence or chaos in the creation tends towards acceptance of violence as normative for the

---

[21] Imprecatory Psalms and other 'curse my enemy pieces' display the very human aspect of the scripture. These pieces can also reflect the desire of a suffering person for their oppressors to know the depth of pain they feel in their suffering so that their oppressors would cease to cause such harm. In this sense suffering has the potential to both destroy us and to increase our humanity.

human experience. However, the call of God to humanity is to resist violence. In order to end violence, we must learn to study the scripture's instruction on violence as originating with human beings.

Violence is indigenous to the human condition, but rejecting violence is to reach for God. This is so because God is calling humanity to an existence without death.

Violence in scripture begins in the human action to reach beyond the underlying structures of reality, to reach for immortality at the expense of life in the present. Next is the violence we do to one another through scapegoating, to blame rather than take responsibility for our failed actions. Then violence is portrayed as mimetic rivalry: the desire to take the place of the other. In Genesis polygamy and the abuse of women for sex and breeding culminates in religiously condoned violence and in the eruption of chaos in the natural world.[22]

Accepting violence as inevitable allowed Israel to think that God both tolerated and sanctioned violence. The monotheism of Israel draws God into all facets of life, including the human propensity to resort to war and horrific violence. Since God's mercy allows human beings to live in spite of their violence, then God is free

---

[22] The movements of violence in scripture are depicted in Eve's reach for the fruit, then Adam's blaming of God, Eve's blaming the serpent and in Adam's case also indirectly blaming Eve; to blame when guilty is to scapegoat. The next is Cain's mimetic desire to replace or remove Abel rather than change. Lamech, the first polygamist invokes God to justify his taking of two wives and threatens them if they challenge his actions. The flood is creation's response to the violence of breeding through the taking of women by powerful men.

to work within the constraints of human violence.[23] This view holds God accountable for all outcomes and so voids chance and human responsibility. In effect, Israel blames God for everything and credits God for everything. If they think violence is a viable solution, then God is approving of said solution.

Often, writing that the Lord spoke to Moses is more the theological conclusion of a scribe than an actual fact; even attributing to Moses verbal commands for violence is literary theology rather than historical accuracy. Or, it can be that the voice of Moses in the text is occasionally the view of the people because they cannot comprehend the ways of a world without violence - the way of nonviolent resistance. At these moments in the text, Moses the man is separated from Moses the figurehead, whose governing word is presented as totalitarian rule, rather than received as instructive. Torah is always more about 'teaching' and mercy than literal execution.

The story of Phinehas portrays Moses' leadership as both figurehead and as a powerfully powerless person.

The view of God as wrathful and angry is the outcome of God's absence. Meaning God does not protect Israel from her enemies because God has left them to their own doings. God's absence is equated with anger. When God does not protect Israel and lets others defeat them,

---

[23] For example, although God is free to determine the outcome of a war it is apparent in scripture that God does not make this a consistent practice. God was drawn into a war with Pharaoh, but in the destruction of the Northern Kingdom and in the exile of the Southern Kingdom it is God's absence that allowed the horror and terror that came against Israel.

then they look for a cause, something that in their mind angered God. The presence of death - an epidemic, a plague - is viewed as an act of God's anger. If anything bad happens Israel thinks God is angry. Israel does not know God as the easily grieved Spirit, as the Prince of peace. Reading the OT requires a person to acknowledge the progressive work of God's self-revelation in history, and the projection of humanity's failed self-control upon religious claims about God.[24]

The progressive revelation of God in the scriptures does not mean that God matures, but that the revelation of God's self through interaction with Israel, the prophets, and humanity, requires a story. It is a story that culminates in the life and person of Jesus Christ, who is the defining revelation of God. So, all perceptions of God in the OT are made clear (not contradicted) in Christ Jesus. It is my conviction and experience that all readings of scripture can be presented as instructive for overcoming violence and so revealing God as non-violent and merciful (*hesed*).

In the midst of competing theological ideologies, there were scribal geniuses whose narrative efforts preserve the tension caused by inconsistencies in biblical stories for theological and anthropological reasons. Or, the genius that I perceive is the Spirit of God working through humanity's triumphs and failures to provide lessons, and revelation; the beauty of an undiscovered land of shalom.

---

[24] Humanity's failed self-control is the inability to identify the systemic structures of human psychology and socio-cultural formation that inhibit understanding of the forces through which we view reality. These 'principalities' are mimetic desire, the ideology of violence as inevitable, and forming God in our image rather than fulfilling the image of God in us.

The book of Numbers appears to be the human voice of Israel attempting to identify the voice of both God and Moses when both God and Moses have become silent in a self-imposed absence due to the stiff-necked state of a generation. In the silence of God and Moses, the institutionalized violence of religious priests with a history of vying for power claims to speak for God and Moses.

Setting the Stage

The supportive back-story that precedes the story of Phinehas in Numbers 25 is the story of Balaam. This story offers the reader a view of how God works behind the scenes to protect Israel, to ensure that Israel is not destroyed. In the Phinehas story, it looks as though God would kill all of Israel in a plague if not for the actions of Phinehas the priest. This is inconsistent with God's purposes for Israel.

Terror and the Vigilante

Numbers chapter 25 is a story that credits a priest (Phinehas) with saving Israel from the counsel of Balaam. The counsel of Balaam was a plan to infect the men of Israel with a 'plague' of idolatry. The initial reading of the text allows for other possibilities for understanding the plague. The plague might be understood as a sexually transmitted disease or some other contagious virus, or they were poisoned during meals offered to Chemosh (Numbers 25:2). However, an STD cannot account for the rapid deaths recorded. Such a plague would endanger the Moabites / Midianites as well. A slow poisoning during meals in Moabite temples is unlikely because the plague is presented as immediate.

It is more likely that the plague is representative of the death reflected in the exclusion of Idolaters from the life and God of Israel. So death is not literal but an ideological plague. This is consistent with the end of the wilderness generation upon the conclusion of chapter twenty-five and the beginning story of the next generation in chapter 26.

It is reasonable to think that Balaam's counsel was to destroy the power of their religious culture with the temptation to idolatry.[25] I think Balaam knew this generation of Israelites had been secluded to the wilderness wanderings for their failure to be faithful to the monotheism of Yahweh. Balaam also knows that sexually restrained males are easily seduced and subject to the influence of relationships with 'foreign' women.

It is important to note that the Israelite males failed to teach the Moabite women the stories and revelation of Yahweh that belonged to their history. These males were, in a sense, the plague, because they did not believe and adopted idolatrous beliefs (Hebrews 3:19). The tendency of reading the text to put the blame on the foreign women as seductresses is to ignore the responsibility of Israelite males.

Chapter twenty-five of Numbers begins with a command for an act of terror, allegedly at the behest of Yhwh and Moses. Israel has descended to a point where acts of terror against her own people are portrayed as religiously sanctioned practice. Chapter 25 marks the end of a generation; the first census begins the story of the generation refused entry into the land. The second census (ch.26) is of the next generation who are to

---

[25] See Numbers 31:16 and Revelation 2:14 Balaam counseled Balak on how to defeat Israel in spite of Balaam's oracles.

inherit the land. Terror, sex, idolatry, and a vigilante priest mark the contents of chapter 25.

The anger of the Lord is a product of Israelite males engaging in sex with Moabite women, eating at their temples and particularly for bowing down to their gods. The family oriented endogamy of the patriarchs was unsustainable as a practice. The practice of requiring a tribal oriented endogamy is likewise unsustainable.[26] Israel's problem with embracing these cross-cultural relationships is the ensuing idolatry by a generation of males who have rejected the voice of God consistently throughout their wilderness wanderings; the Moabite women were not the problem. The failure of the male Israelites to serve the one God (Yahweh) is the problem.

In contrast to the patriarchal endogamy supported by Priestly theology is an abundance of counter stories. Moses' wife was a Midianite. Ruth is a competing or counter story for categorizing Moabite women as void of value. Naomi taught Ruth; the Israelite males failed to teach their Moabite women. Someone taught Rahab, the harlot of Jericho, and she is listed in the genealogy of Jesus. The stream of priestly theology that flows through the Old Testament is in conflict with the Deuteronomist stream of theology that is compatible with both the prophets and the teaching of Jesus.[27]

---

[26] The violence of Nehemiah and Ezra towards those persons who were mixed with the people of the lands was evidence of their cruel religious reform that ultimately failed. Both men were building a political and religious institution on practices of exclusion rather than the teaching of scripture.

[27] Priestly theology is institutional, national, militaristic and functions through symbols and ceremony rather than storytelling

The sexual impropriety of the Israelite males and females took place throughout the wilderness wanderings; you can't put everyone to death! The death penalty in Israel was written more as instructive for readers of the text than it was for practical application during the wilderness wanderings, or any other period of time in human history. Meaning that the death penalty is representative of the presence of death in the violations of Torah from a purely legal standpoint; mercy and forgiveness are always available. This understanding of the text as written for 'us' and not for those who lived through these experiences is an imperative for solid interpretive theology.

The rhetoric of Israel's leaders (particularly priests) is found in these narratives from Numbers. Often memories from a distant past are preserved with stories that seek to explain the present and strike fear into dissidents. Stories like Numbers chapter twenty-five in a cursory reading claim the preservation of Israel's distinctiveness as the people of God was sustained through priestly violence. [28] Priestly violence must be identified as virtuous if it

---

and compassion, traits that belong to the Deuteronomist. The Deuteronomist seeks to establish egalitarian justice maintained by a change of heart, whereas the Priestly seeks to establish a hierarchy of socio-political religious power through legalism.

[28] Exodus 32:26-29; the function of the story is to communicate that the priesthood is bestowed upon the sons of Levi who kill their own family members in their zeal for Yhwh. In effect the members of the Levitical priesthood are violent men and part of the purpose of the priesthood is to restrain their violence. This portion of the story in Exodus 32 is inconsistent with the surrounding events. Moses has discerned the voice of God as willing to let the people all perish in their self-destructive idolatry. We learn that God is not in a hurry and is willing to start over with Moses. When Moses views the debauchery of the people, their nakedness, then Moses vs. 30

is to be legitimized. Violence in the priestly narratives is a normalized practice when it is for the sake of zealousness. The priestly voice is misaligned with God and will be challenged by prophets. Prophets like Moses will stand-alone and intercede for the people; others will compromise and seek approval from the practitioners of violence in the religious-state apparatus. Levitical religion with its priests and sacrificial system was born because the people rejected God's voice at the mountain.

The initial act of terror in this piece is the command to execute certain leaders whose bodies are to be left on open display, allegedly to turn away the anger of God. The command to execute the 'chiefs' places culpability upon them for the actions of those males (young men) who compromise their belief in the one God for the idolatrous beliefs of the Moabite women. The 'chiefs' have not passed on the faith; death is upon them for their failure.

The command to execute is given by Moses (in the text). The judges are to fulfill the command. Would the judges even have the power to fulfill such a command? The command is never fulfilled; it is averted by the actions of Phinehas. The anger of the Lord is manifested in an unidentified plague whose origin is connected to the practice of table fellowship in the temples of the Midianite / Moabite peoples. It is not a horrific display of executed

---

returns to meet with Yhwh in order to insist that Yhwh must forgive them or Moses cannot continue on with God; that is Moses chooses annihilation over living with a God that does not forgive. Moses intercedes for the people on both sides of the priestly story (26-29) and displays the true function of a priest (and Prophet). Genesis 49:5-7 records the cursed violence of Simeon and Levi. The sons of Levi cannot be restrained unless they are allowed to practice some form of (alleged) redemptive or virtuous violence.

leaders that halts the plague, but the alleged virtuous violence of Aaron's grandson Phinehas. It seems that Levitical religion is sustainable only through violence.

The plague claimed the lives of twenty-four thousand persons before Phinehas' slaying of an Israelite male and a Midianite woman took place. Moses and the people were weeping before the tent over both the ensuing loss of life (the execution command) and the display of terror (impaling the chiefs and slaughtering idolaters) to be accomplished by the judges. Moses' presence with the people weeping at the tabernacle makes his participation in commanding the slaying and public display of horror unlikely, unless Moses knew it would not be followed through. It is notable that he does not seem to have the power to accomplish the command. If this were the case then the command is more communication on the end result of idolatry than actual administration of capital punishment. The plague is not mentioned until verse eight.

While Moses and the people are weeping at the tabernacle over the command for a public execution in order to avert the anger of Yhwh, Phinehas' rises to slay the Israelite male and the Midianite woman. His killing is credited with halting the plague and the public execution. Phinehas is with Moses and the people before the tabernacle when he rises to slay Zimri and Cozbi. It seems comical to think that people are dying by the thousands, yet Zimri and Cozbi are unmoved by those events and continue in an uninhibited display of relationship. The two murdered young people are named because they come from well-known families (Numbers 25:14). The relationship of Zimri and Cozbi depicts a mature, consensual, and legitimate relationship of young people from established families.

Phinehas' killing is motivated as a response to the command for capital punishment to be inflicted upon the elders of the group of Idolaters. Phinehas' actions allegedly halt the executions (if they were ever going to take place). That Phinehas' actions avoid the fulfillment of the command and end the plague questions the absoluteness of a command of Yahweh or Moses to put the idolaters to death. The deaths in the plague are to be read in light of the end of a generation (of males) refused entrance into the land. Their death is solidified as certain; any hope for a merciful change of heart from God is ended. Without hope, death is already accomplished.

The violent nature of sacrificial religion affects the practitioners. The bible fills the priesthood with the children of Levi, a people characterized as violent prior to being appointed as priests (Genesis 49:5-7). Their tendency to violence is constrained by ritual sacrifice. Sacrificial religion limits violence because it seeks to make violence a virtue that utilizes scapegoats (Zimri and Cozbi). In this case, the use of terror through public violence (the act of Phinehas), killing socially elite persons who are usually exempt from punishment, strikes fear into all others.

Ritual sacrifice offers a temporary release or a symbolic substitute for the building tendency of human desire to resort to violence as a solution.[29] Nonetheless, sacrificial religion is violence-oriented and sacrifice is insufficient to constrain violence, thus it erupts in alleged virtuous violence through sanctioned acts like the story of Phinehas. Sacrificial religion also projects the human

---

[29] Penal Substitution Theory is blight on Christian faith. The perceived wrath of God is the absence of God in the present. God was forgiving sins long before Jesus and not on credit! John 3:16 is clear, the cross was an act of love, a revelation of God.

propensity to violence and the ritual of sacrifice upon the deity, creating a god after their own deficiencies.

Phinehas' victims are remembered by name. The Israelite male, Zimri, was a Simeonite. In relation to Jacob's pronouncements on his sons (Simeon and Levi), the violence of the two brother's descendants is differentiated. Simeon's violence is harmful and Levi's violence is virtuous. Phinehas is honored with a 'covenant of peace' and a 'covenant of everlasting priesthood' for his killing of Zimri and Cozbi the Midianite woman. The final verse of Numbers twenty-five points to cunning trickery by the Midianites that led to the murder of Cozbi on the day of the plague.[30]

The commands in verses 1-5 are not followed through on, the reader is relieved and the writer would like Phinehas' act to be placed in a positive light. In the end, (verses 16-18) Phinehas has successfully made the Moabites and Midianites enemies of Israel without any hope for living with peace. Cozbi is identified as a 'figurehead' and representative of the plan between Balak and Balaam. This use of Cozbi as a figurehead is linked to the use of Moses as a figurehead in the first five verses. In both cases,

---

[30] It seems reasonable to understand the Midianite trickery to be the facilitation of a mixed marriage that would unite the Israelites to the Midianites. The failure of Zimri to teach Cozbi about Israel's faith is indicative of ensuing religious syncretism. This is the fear that birthed the violence of Phinehas. Teaching is set in contrast to religious violence in the story of Zimri and Cozbi. The acts of God experienced by the wilderness generation should have produced people eager to share their story and their God.

the priestly caste is asserting authority as interpreters of 'Moses', that is the Pentateuch.[31]

Wrestling with Scribes

Redaction criticism seeks to identify the editing of scripture by noting distinctive theological prejudices. Jeremiah noted this problem and rejected the editorial efforts of scribes as a corruption of God's intent; as a lie. Jeremiah knows people read scripture literally and do not question the formative work of Israel's scribes. Religion appeals to the psyche of human beings and defies our finer attributes of reason, study, and morality.

> *How can you say,*
> *"We are wise, and the law of the LORD is with us,"*
> *when, in fact, the false pen of the scribes*
> *has made it into a lie?*
> *(Jeremiah 8:8 NRS)*

The bias of a priestly hand has taken this story and used it for multiple reasons.[32] However, for us, it is the final form canonical status of scripture that requires a person to wrestle with the morality and incongruities in the text. There is value in every piece of scripture. Scripture is

---

[31] Jesus' interpretation of the law of Moses challenged the reading of the Pharisees in John 8. Jesus call for the first stone to be thrown by a person without sin requires a reading of the death penalty refrain as instructive and not to be followed literally. The absence of the guilty male in the story is striking, that this fact is not mentioned leaves Jesus to be viewed as a protector of women from male domination.

[32] The redaction of Numbers in an effort to support traditions concerning the priesthood of Phinehas is a well-established feature of biblical studies in both Judaism and Christianity.

instructive and requires interpretive efforts that reveal or uncover truths about God and humanity, without accepting violence as normative.

Through wrestling with the text, this piece of scripture is revealing of a belief system that supports the idea of virtuous violence and religious zeal. Zealotry and violence are united as honorable, and originating in a person given an eternal priesthood. As a story, it leaves us with the haunting picture of a priest driving a javelin through the bodies of a man and a woman. The man and woman are from notable families in both communities. Their relationship from their perspective seems to be mature and consensual rather than an illicit affair. This is noted in their freedom to meet in the Israelite camp and enter a tent together without fear.

The story's terrifying approval, honoring a priest for an act of horrific violence (apparently, both Cozbi and Zimri were struck through while embracing one another), is shocking. In the text, the horrific act of Phinehas is justified based upon its power to end the plague. However, it is no longer safe for a Midianite woman to have a relationship with an Israelite male. It is the fear of priests who are religious zealots that functions to end the 'wiles' of Midianite (Moabite) leaders. Perhaps Phinehas' murder of the children of powerful families on both sides ended any further hostilities? Phinehas' covenant of peace is a false statement, the view of a priestly writer. His everlasting covenant has not survived; except as the manifestation of sanctioned religious violence, a type of violence not subject to law.

The zealotry of religious violence marks the world with the continuance of a false promise, a promise of shalom built on religious sacrifice. Religious violence becomes a tool for terror, a power for totalitarian regimes; it 'lies' at the heart of empire. Empire seeks to appeal to the religious zeal of the people, to commandeer the voice of God. The opening commands of Numbers 25:1-5 reflect this effort to commandeer the voice of God so that violent men may reign over the people without being subject to the law. I read verses 1-5 as priestly propaganda speaking according to their misguided understandings of Moses' teachings.

Moses is portrayed as a powerless weeping intercessor and he does not want his own command fulfilled. Portrayals of God in the Old Testament are always subject to the revelation of God in Jesus. God is holy, God's character firm and immovable, any inconsistencies with God in the OT and God in the NT are to be exposed through interpretive theology.

A Story: Learning Non-Violent Response

In 1985 the political environment of the Philippines was turbulent and fueled by the people's movement that sought to remove the dictator Ferdinand Marcos from power. I had been traveling and living in areas where the armed resistance movements were active. The comfort of being an American in the Philippines was no longer present.

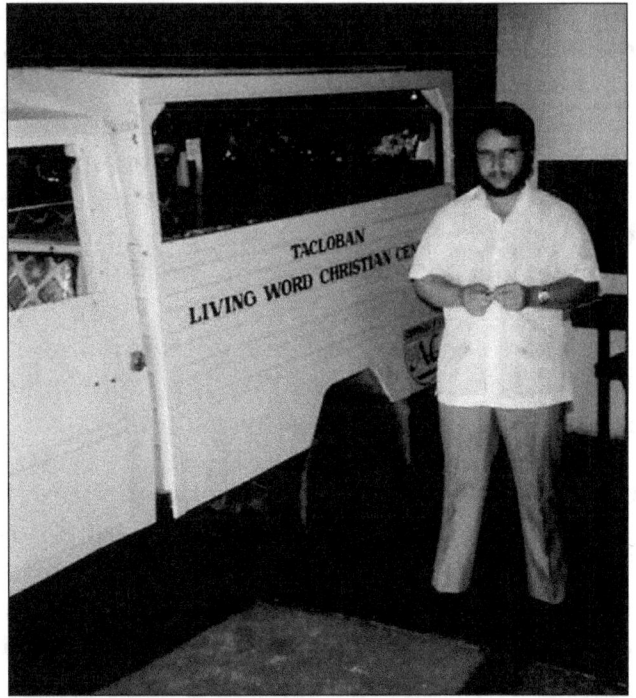

The Jeep in this picture is the one I was driving in the following story. I purchased it with my tax return from working the previous year in the family plumbing business.

Courage or Sorrow

The following incident happened in Leyte. The NPA (New People's Army) was active throughout Leyte and Samar. The dictator Ferdinand Marcos was losing his grip on power, and growing protest against U.S. military presence in the Philippines was daily news. Thankfully, the nation was saved from escalating violence by the non-violent people's movement. The people's movement was a product of Liberation

Theology taught by Catholic priests and lay persons, and practiced in BEC's (Basic Ecclesial Communities).

In 1985 I was driving down a dirt road in the Barangay Sagkahan located just outside of Tacloban City, Leyte. I was in my little multi-cab jeep. My wife and I were seated in the front. In the back, on the benches, were my three children and our two Filipina helpers. We were driving home from church. Each Sunday I held services in a conference room at Leyte College. This particular Sunday a young man had brought his gun to our service. After hearing the preaching he informed me that he was returning it to the NPA and was going to serve Jesus.

As we were driving home, out of the thick vegetation, jumped a sunburnt man wearing only shorts and yielding a stone larger than a softball. He propelled the stone with all the strength he had and it hit the side of my jeep. I was unable to drive fast because the road was busy with street vendors and playing children. The man grabbed another stone and I did not want my children to be struck, so I stopped the jeep. If I had continued driving he would have had a clear trajectory into the back of the jeep and might have hit one of my children or one of the girls.

As I stepped out of the jeep, he asked me if I was an American (Americano Ca). In the Waray language, he said he was going to kill me with his stone. I had no choice but to rush towards him, as I moved quickly to stop him from throwing the stone. I responded in the Waray language and told him he had better not miss. He decided to run. He quickly out-ran me and disappeared in a nearby village. I was going to return to my family when I noticed some people looking rather troubled gazing into their backyard. Thinking he was hiding I went over to the yard. During all of this commotion, I noticed one of our helpers named Lyn Lyn was following me. I knew she was there to ensure my safety. She was a bright girl and alert to my cultural differences. To this day we remain friends with Lyn. She and her husband assist my students and friends from G.O.D. International.

I walked over to the small group of men and women staring into a vegetable garden behind a small Nipa home. There he was, crouched down in the midst of the growing rows of the family's garden. Well, he was not a man carrying an M-16 rifle like the members of the NPA whom I had hidden from on my trips to Southern Leyte. He was just a poor skinny man whose lips were white with hunger. Lyn Lyn said, "Manong, he is hungry, see his lips are white". I looked at him, his glass-like gaze and red-colored eyes filled with pain, he reached into the plants and began to eat raw vegetables.

Returning to my jeep, I thought how only minutes earlier I was prepared to use violence to stop this poor, lonely, hungry man. I wish I could tell you that I left him some gift, but in the moment I was concerned for the welfare of my family and events like this were fairly common. If I had been more mature, if I had been less stressed, if I had more financial support, I think I would have aided the poor man with food and clothing. This is not a story about courage, it is a story about sorrow and suffering, it is a reflection of how we all must navigate our way through a complex and troubled world. It is about my failure to respond with greater love. I didn't feel courageous after this event, rather; I felt a deep need to be more sensitive in the midst of conflict. I felt as though I had missed an opportunity to help one of Lazarus' children, one of God's children.

Chapter III

The Absence of God

God, Violence, Absence, and Culpability in Hosea

Preparing the Reader

Initially, the narrator introduces the book of Hosea supplying two important aspects for communicating how the reader is to receive the words of the book of Hosea. First, the word of Yahweh is set in a certain time period and delivered to a certain man. So, determining universal applications of these words of Hosea is dependent upon understanding the limits of a historical experience and a particular man. Second, the writings that follow the account of Hosea's life are a product of the man's obedience to a personal command, a command that disrupts his life. He is to take a harlot and make her his wife. It is conceivable within the text that she had children prior to her marriage to Hosea, and others were born and named afterward.[33] In Hosea, God speaks

---

[33] When the LORD first spoke through Hosea, the LORD said to Hosea, "Go, take for yourself a wife of whoredom and have children of whoredom, for the land commits great whoredom by forsaking the LORD." The word have is a translators addition, this can easily read 'take a wife and children of whoredom'. Likewise the word 'brother' and 'sister' in Hosea's speech to Jezreel in 2:1 are both

through the ruptured soul of a man whose experiences and thoughts are presented as the word of Yahweh.

The first three chapters provide the reader with a brief account of Hosea's private life as a public sign for communicating the speech and pathos of God. Like a vessel of clay, Hosea's life has been formed for communicating the heart of God. Although Hosea's life has been torn apart by betrayal and deep emotional pain, he will not release the God who has held his life captive to love and heartache; nor will God release Hosea.

God speaks and God's speech is mixed up in the life and emotions of Hosea.[34] Hosea will speak for God through God speeches that lack the introductory formula, 'thus says the LORD'. The flow of thought between Hosea's words and God's speeches are not separated by the power of a speech formula. God's and Hosea's views on reality are inseparable. Hosea puts flesh to the word in the sense that God is not allowed to hide. Hosea brings God into the world through a life aligned with the desire and pain of God. God enters our world through Hosea's speech and writings. The consequence of God's inaction (absence) is named by Hosea as God's actions. God's inaction, God's departing, God's absence, is understood as anger. Is God an angry lover?

---

plural in Hebrew, meaning there were other children besides Jezreel, Lo-Ammi and Lo-Ruhamah.

[34] Hechel's well known saying fits well with my thoughts; "I would say the prophet is a man who is able to hold God and man in one thought, at one time, at all times". See: Heschel, Abraham Joshua *Moral Grandeur and Spiritual Audacity*, (U.S.A.: Farrar, Straus and Giroux, 1996) pg. 399.

Hope Pieces

Interspersed throughout the book of Hosea are 'hope pieces'.[35] These prophetic utterances of hope provide the reader with a view of God's desire in contrast to God's actions. God is not allowed to experience God's hope for the object of his love. This is so because the people are not like God; only Hosea is like, or, knows God. The rift between God and the object of his desire is Hosea's story of a one-sided love affair. Hosea knows this pain; he has been commanded to take a wife of harlotry. This has touched his family, a family with children not belonging to Hosea. Hosea's entire life is a sign act of experiential metaphor for the pathos of God in relation to Israel.

Absence Violence and Culpability

It is my purpose to produce a fluid presentation on the major theological theme that pervades the book of Hosea and draw from it teaching that challenges perceptions of God as violent. This theme is the absence of God. The absence of God is portrayed in Hosea as anger. I do not intend to exclude the tension present in the text where the reality of violence seeks resolve; resolving the problem of evil is beyond the scope of my effort.

The absence of God is a theological theme that is mixed with the culpability of God. Meaning, although God leaves human beings and nation states to suffer the consequences of their choices and the choices of other persons or nations, God is aware of how we perceive God to be in the world. God's absence in the biblical texts speaks from a human

---

[35] Hope pieces in Hosea are 1:10-11; 2:14-23; 3:5; 6:1-3; 11:10-11; 14:1-9.

perspective with metaphors and in poetic form. Like Job, Hosea holds God accountable for reality.

The following two verses bracket verses 7-14. Verse 6 is the author (Hosea) speaking. Verse 15 is a God speech that sits as a dance partner in relation to verse 6; the dance is the verses in-between. The verses in-between utilize metaphors drawn from nature that depict God as being 'like' maggots and 'like' a lion killing to return later and eat. In God's absence the natural world 'speaks'.[36] If you will, the practice of wisdom is to discern the voice of God in the natural world. However, through the use of poetry and metaphor the prophets separate God from the 'voice' or 'wisdom' that reflect God's role as creator; God is more than creation reveals. The revelation of God in creation is limited. For this reason, redemption has a history.

⁶ With their flocks and herds they shall go to seek the LORD,
but they will not find him;
he has withdrawn from them.
(Hosea 5:6)

I will return again to my place until they acknowledge their guilt and seek my face.
In their distress they will beg my favor:
(Hosea 5:15)

---

[36] The poem at the end of Hosea 2 provides 'voice' for the creation's relation to God. Not in a literal way, this is why it is in poetry. Hosea 2: 21-23 *On that day I will answer, says the LORD, I will answer the heavens and they shall answer the earth; and the earth shall answer the grain, the wine, and the oil, and they shall answer Jezreel; and I will sow him for myself in the land. And I will have pity on Lo-ruhamah, and I will say to Lo-ammi, "You are my people"; and he shall say, "You are my God."*

Hosea introduces the absence of God in verse 6. In the absence of God, hope becomes a poem, a longing for God. Violence becomes a reality brought upon Israel by God's inaction. God will now be experienced as 'maggots' and 'rottenness'. Further, God will be to Judah like a young lion that tears and goes away.[37] In the absence of God, creation fails and humanity is not restrained from horrific acts of terror.

In the absence of God, Israel suffers the loss of divine protection and expansionist powers will devour her. Due to rampant immorality and idolatry, the land will not flourish and her people will suffer. It would be a mistake to suppose that all suffering people are marked as rejected groups subjected to the judgment of God. God allows unrestrained evil to prevail in human history and the suffering of the righteous also occurs. Israel's prophets spoke within the context of a revelatory historical work of God. Israel's story is our story; it is a reflection of all humanity. How God is discerned in the flow of history, in the torrents of powers constructed by men, is the effort of Israel's prophets. The absence of God in history is the absence of God in humanity.[38] In the book of Hosea, God is not present with either the Assyrians or the Israelites. What is God doing?

---

[37] I am of the opinion that the writings of Hosea were edited to apply the message of Hosea to Judah at a later date.

[38] The prophet Amos clarifies that God works in the history of other peoples. Yet the revelatory nature of God's promises to Jacob will not fail; God's hope abides and God will win over the people of God. See *Amos 9:7*. *⁷Are you not like the Ethiopians to me, O people of Israel? says the LORD. Did I not bring Israel up from the land of Egypt, and the Philistines from Caphtor and the Arameans from Kir?*

God's Conflicted Questions:

> *⁴ What shall I do with you, O Ephraim?*
> *What shall I do with you, O Judah?*
> (Hosea 6:4)

Is God conflicted? Do God's creatures place God in a position of unknowing? Is our potential for forming reality so grand as to sit at the precipice of eternity and choose an unknown possibility? Through Moses and the prophets, God has been revealing God's self and longing to make the entire nation (people) of Israel as a sign act to all nations, all humanity.[39] God's relationship with Israel was uniquely different than any other group or nation of people. Their failure is our failure, their story our story. God will be required to give more of God's self in order to fulfill God's desire for humanity. The distance between creator and creature will need more work, more time. God is still hidden in the realm of difference.

God's response:

> *⁶ For I desire steadfast love and not sacrifice,*
> *the knowledge of God rather than burnt offerings.*
> (Hosea 6:6)

Out of this intense poetic piece of broken relationship, the dialogue continues. God speaks and bursts asunder all of Israel's perceptions of the relationship between God and humanity. God desires to be loved – to be known. Love is relational and knowledge is intimate.

---

[39] *Deuteronomy 4:6 ⁶ You must observe them diligently, for this will show your wisdom and discernment to the peoples, who, when they hear all these statutes, will say, "Surely this great nation is a wise and discerning people!"*

The constructs of religious practice built upon sacrifice and offerings are empty, it leaves the soul untouched. God has shown his love through a man who loved a woman, who loved the children she bore, who loved as his heart was ripped open and his life shamed – a prophet married to an adulterous woman.[40]

The tension over God's culpability in relation to God's absence is built into the God speeches of the prophets. Do the prophets grasp a benevolent being that can be both emotional yet self-controlled? Or, do they refuse to let God off the hook so easily! So, the Torah and the Prophets and the Writings all have moments where God is so mixed up in the present reality that in spite of God's absence - God cannot be absent; God must be angry. God is held culpable for existence by the prophets and cannot engage in hiding or leaving unless he is angry. God is held accountable for reality even as God is holding Israel (humanity) accountable for reality.

Apart from anger, how else are human beings to understand the horrible events that take place when God is absent and humanity is left to her own devices? On the one hand, we are made aware of humanity's great need for God, on the other, we resist the idea of God's absence and God escaping culpability as unacceptable – we hold God to account for the existence of suffering.[41]

---

[40] We shouldn't get lost in the associated gender problems presented in the relationship of Hosea and Gomer; we are all Gomer, male and female.

[41] God is guilty of being merciful and God's culpability for human existence is revealed on a cross. The wrestling of God and humanity is the story of God's merciful redeeming work and self-giving love.

God cannot let go of humanity and the prophets cannot let go of either God or humanity. The lives and speeches of the prophets bring God into the world like God brings the prophets into the world.

Conflicted Again

> *⁸ How can I give you up, Ephraim?*
> *How can I hand you over, O Israel?*
> *How can I make you like Admah?*
> *How can I treat you like Zeboiim?*
> *My heart recoils within me;*
> *my compassion grows warm and tender.*
> *⁹ I will not execute my fierce anger;*
> *I will not again destroy Ephraim;*
> *for I am God and no mortal, the Holy One in your midst,*
> *and I will not come in wrath.*
> *(Hosea 11:8-9)*

God does not have a shadow side![42] God has work to do in order to lift up from the ground the human beings that God has created. The greatest aspect of that work is to reveal God's self to the creature (humanity) who bears his image (the potential to be 'like' God). The tension in the second conflict poem reveals God as one who seeks a way to consummate his relationship of love and intimacy with humanity.

It is revelatory of God's desire to be known intimately beyond the constructs of raw power to the beauty of inward holiness.

[42] C.F. Jung reads the scripture in such a way that he insists upon a God in process who must overcome his 'dark side'. Jung's error is he places God in process rather than revelation (the revelatory process).

The temporary moment of absence that has depicted God as angry is brought into question. The poetic God speech accepts that God's actions have been understood as anger. However, the presence of God is not marked by wrath, his absence is marked by wrath. God is not a human being, is not vengeful; this is why vengeance belongs to God. God is not subject to fits of rage or a lack of self-control.

God will come, and not in wrath; wrath or anger is humanity's view of God when God departs. The tension in Hosea that accepts humanity's, or the prophet's view of God over against the view of a non-violent God is measured up in a demand for culpability. God's culpability will come over the course of redemptive history.

Hope's End is God's Victory

The final chapter of Hosea in its entirety is a hope piece. It is expressive of a time to come, a time when God has won over the hearts of humanity through God's progressive self-revelation in redemptive history. God will no longer be perceived as angry for God will not depart, God will not be absent from reality.

Hosea depicts receiving the constant presence of God as dependent upon the people of God. Verse 3 represents the fruit of their lips. It is the turning point in human history when humanity is embraced into the being (Spirit) of God.

> *³ Assyria shall not save us;*
> *we will not ride upon horses;*
> *we will say no more, 'Our God,' to the work of our hands.*
> *In you the orphan finds mercy."*
> Hosea 14:3

Verse three is humanity refusing to pursue empire, refusing to practice war and no longer reaching beyond the structures of reality set in place by God. Orphaned by God's absence, humanity has found mercy.

This prayer in Hosea 14:3 is not mere words to repeat or hope only to come when God acts with finality. Rather, this prayer is admonishment for the present. Often the hope pieces are models for living in the present; models that bring God into the world.

This prayer of Hosea is as important as the Lord's Prayer in the gospels. The prayer addresses the perennial idols interspersed in the commentary section on the Decalogue in Deuteronomy (ch.7-9). The idol of materialism is the appealing wealth of Assyria that cannot save. The refusal of the idol of militarism is to reject the horses of war. The idol of nationalism is broken before the God of all the earth. Israel will become a people, the people of God, even the children of God.

READINGS

IN

NON-SACRAMENTAL THEOLOGY

Part Two:

NON-SACRAMENTAL THEOLOGY

Introduction

The primary tenet of non-sacramental theology is that in the eyes of God, human beings alone are sacred. This is followed by the weighted reality behind all biblical law, which is the preservation of life. Life, of course, is subject to moral decision-making, which can be very complicated in a world where God's reign is disrupted by human desire and device.

It is my understanding that God alone is Holy in the sense that holiness is God's nature and God cannot be other than who God is. We must partake of the divine nature if we are to be holy.

Thus he has given us, through these things, his precious and very great promises, so that through them you may escape from the corruption that is in the world because of lust, and may become participants of the divine nature.
(2Pet. 1:4)

For this reason, holiness ascribed to any person or object is always by association. Of course, an object cannot truly be sacred. It is for this reason that Moses' bones were hidden. People tend to ascribe holiness to dead bodies and graves of deceased leaders. Desecration of such a place usually requires the death of the offender. In such a case, the value of the life of the offender is less than that of a tomb with dead bones. This can never be so in God's eyes. A marble tomb taking up space on a hill over a beautiful bay is an ignorant display of vanity. Beautifully preserved graves and graveyards sit in contrast to the masses of people in the world living in hovels of poverty.[43]

Jeremiah is the prince of deconstructing ideas about the enduring inviolability of buildings, land, symbols, and objects. I suppose if he were alive today he would have a lot to say about the idea that the Temple Mount is a holy place. The last time he was at the temple he determined that the name of God combined with the Temple constructed a lie. Both scripture and Jewish tradition support the claim that Jeremiah destroyed Israel's ultimate symbol, the Ark of the Covenant.

---

[43] Overlooking Subic Bay from the hilltop below the PREDA Foundation is the gravesite of a dead man in a very large marble box. This gravesite sits alone, displaced from the cemetery; a park bench would have served the living. The preservation of the body in any form is a vain exercise. God does not need any of our decaying flesh to resurrect us for life everlasting. It is good to care for the burial or cremation of a human body. Moses was seen at the transfiguration while his bones had long before returned to the dust of the earth. Remembering the life lived by those who have passed should be done in a story, not in an attempt at permanently housing their body.

> *Do not trust in these lying words, saying,*
> *"Temple Yahweh, Temple Yahweh, Temple Yahweh."*
> *(Jeremiah 7:4)*[44]

> *And when you have multiplied and increased in the land,*
> *in those days, says the LORD, they shall no longer say,*
> *"The ark of the covenant of the LORD."*
> *It shall not come to mind, or be remembered, or missed;*
> *nor shall another one be made.*
> *(Jer. 3:16)*

It is well known that the Gospel of John spiritualizes the communion ceremony and on the night of Jesus' Passover meal the ceremony is replaced by the practical need for Peter to have his dirty feet washed and his pride excoriated by Jesus' act of humility. In the gospel of John, Jesus' baptism is not recorded and it is explicitly stated that Jesus baptized no one. Paul seems disinterested in baptism and remembers two persons, but does not even remember the names of a household of people whom he apparently baptized. Paul's attitude toward baptism is that it is lived out as a life immersed into the death of Jesus, a death to all the violence that forms the present human reality.

> *For Christ did not send me to baptize but to proclaim the gospel, and not with eloquent wisdom, so that the cross of Christ might not be emptied of its power.*
> *(1ˢᵗ Corinthians 1:17)*

---

[44] The impact of the two words 'Temple Yahweh' heard by the Hebrews is more impactful than utilizing the English construct. The odd phrasing of 'the these' at the end of the verse I placed in the first sentence with the word 'these', this order is more suited to the English speaking ears.

It is important when reading the Bible to remember that it records all the errors of God's people, even when they attributed to him speech, command, and approval. It is up to us to bring our morality to the Bible and read it with the awareness that it is about both God and Humanity. It is apparent that human beings like their religion in small doses of pedantic meaning. So, ceremony or sacraments provide actions that require no real challenge to live out the moral demands of Christian faith (Colossians 2:16-17, 23).

While my theological practice is free of ceremony and sacramental activities, there is one area of life where I am tempted to apply the concept of sacrament. This is in regard to the institution of marriage. I am fond of repeating to young people regularly, "Love doesn't come without a promise". The promise before God contained in the marriage ceremony is about as close to creating the sacred as we human beings can get. Human life cannot function without promises, without the legal ramifications of that old-fashioned word 'covenant', a legally binding promise. Of course, a legal agreement doesn't require the relational concept of love and commitment constituted in a marriage vow.

Marriage is unlike religious ceremony; it is a creative force. There is the prospect of children, where we participate in the creation of human beings. There is a God-likeness found in keeping a promise, even when it is extremely difficult. The relational realities of marriage and family form the stability that makes life possible in a way consistent with God's intentions. Watching a healthy spouse remain with an unhealthy spouse, is a sign of love supported by a promise lived out before God.

Marriage can tame sexual desire with all of its endless trappings. Sexuality is always a problem for human beings, in part because we sexualize our speech and refuse constraint. Somewhere between the promise of love and the surety of death lies the power to overcome sexual desire.

Yet, marriage can be annulled if an unbelieving spouse rejects the believing spouse because of their faith. Likewise, because the life of a human being is sacred, if one spouse is endangered by the continuance of the marriage then ending the marriage is advisable. Promiscuity is also a life-endangering practice, both physically (disease) and emotionally. So, marriage is not inviolable (Matthew 19:9).

In our present age when the institution of marriage is facing a 'psychotic episode', attempting to define humanity as other than what we are, the people of God must not fall prey to such contortions of reality. Society's effort to normalize marriage as anything other than a promise between a man and a woman is dependent upon a metaphysical myth. This myth promotes the idea that a 'created' desire for a sexual life with the same sex is the work of God. The myth calls upon evidence for love as further justification for a lifeless sexual union.

If the preservation of life is understood as the underlying effort for all law, then marriage must hold a special place within any Christian community; a place of honor and blessing, a place of promise and love, a place where God works.

Chapter I

The Love Feast and Communion as a Tool for Unity

The church in Corinth is a troublesome group. Paul's letters to this motley bunch of multi-nationals provide a lengthy list of subjects for Christian ethicists. The schismatic persons at the beginning of his first letter seek to divide the group according to some form of celebrity. Each schismatic is identifying himself with recognized personas and claiming some form of authority.

> *What I mean is that each of you says,*
> *"I belong to Paul," or "I belong to Apollos," or*
> *"I belong to Cephas," or "I belong to Christ."*
> *(1st Corinthians 1:2)*

Paul's effort to unite the powerful and the powerless in 1st Corinthians 11 begins with a curious piece about women wearing veils. Not only does Paul want women to wear veils in the church, he wants them to both pray and to prophesy publicly. The liberation of women to speak with *charismata* in public gatherings of believers sits in stark contrast to the command to wear a veil. The cultural practice of wearing a veil in Corinth was to distinguish prostitutes from other women. Women who wore their hair down in public were 'advertising' their availability.

For some, this was their only means of survival; otherwise, their status as slaves left them vulnerable to the wealthy. So, when Paul requires all women to wear veils, he is equalizing women within the Christian meetings. In Greek culture, a 'respectable' woman, whether married or widowed wore a veil.[45]

Paul's use of scripture to support his argument is a product of Greek cultural realities. In the world of Corinth, a woman's hair was linked to sexuality. Paul effectively forms two realities. One is the need to live at peace within a culture and not become an object of persecution over small matters, like a veil. Imagine the joy of a woman not allowed to wear a veil attend a Christian gathering where she is 'required' to wear a veil. The other is to recognize that the worship of God is accomplished in an egalitarian setting where the seed of the Kingdom can flourish and grow to affect the culture. Paul's letters are not 'rule books'; they are occasional responses to the complexities of cross-cultural ministry.

The most divisive power in the Corinthian church is the perennial power of wealth to divide humanity. Paul is dependent upon the wealthy persons; it is they who can read his letters. They have homes where the people can meet. It is their power that enables them to meet pressing needs in the life of the poor and develop their community around education. Nonetheless, there is a division between rich and poor of such threatening proportions that it leads to intolerable practices. These practices led to sickness and even death for some of the members of the church.

---

[45] Ruden, Sarah *Paul Among the People: The Apostle Reinterpreted and Reimagined in His OwnTime* (New York: Random House Publishers, 2010) Pgs. 85-88.

Table Fellowship

Table fellowship has a long tradition in scripture. The practice of hospitality is exhibited in the lives of exemplary figures like Abraham and less favorable characters like Lot. Jesus seems to love feeding people or eating with others, whether they are unacceptable persons, religious persons, crowds, or his friends. Apparently, everyone wanted to have Jesus over for a meal, and Jesus wanted the meals open to everyone!

Love feasts (*agape*) were a common practice in the early church. The fellowship (*koinonia*) around a meal held a role in their worship and was recognized as part of Christian life. The serving of meals to widows was the business of the first 'deacons' and the ministry of the first martyr, Stephen. Table fellowship and hospitality were marks of Hebrew culture and Christian faith.

The Ceremonial Tool

Paul, in an effort to unite the powerful with the powerless, to correct the division of rich and poor, and allow for sharing that brought life to the body of believers in Corinth, utilized the communion ceremony. Paul's solution is to direct the love feast's movement towards worship around the communion ceremony and so end the division in their table fellowship practice. So, Paul's introduction of the ceremony in his letter to the Corinthians was initially more of a tool than later ideas of a sacrament. Initially, the Lord's Supper, in Corinthians is a reference to the agape meal and not the communion ceremony. Note the Lord's supper in the following verses is the meal, it is not the ceremonial piece of bread and single drink of wine.

> *When you come together, it is not really*
> *to eat the Lord's Supper.*
> *For when the time comes to eat, each of you goes*
> *ahead with your own supper,*
> *and one goes hungry and another becomes drunk.*
> *(1st Corinthians 11:20,21)*

His effort to bring the rich and poor together during their table fellowship has several purposes. Paul seeks to sit the rich and poor together at a table where the rich could learn the needs of the poor. This is evident when Paul states that due to the unworthy eating of an agape feast separated from the poor, there had been some members of Christ's body who had suffered both sickness and even death.

The communion ceremony within a love feast serves to include worship of God, conversations about Jesus, and love of the poor through physical provision of needs. The communion ceremony reminds worshippers in the midst of their love feast that humanity kills God, kills their own, and makes victims of the innocent.

The absurd teaching of a self-inflicted curse for partaking unworthily of the elements of the communion ceremony ignores the purpose behind Paul's introduction of the ceremony during a love feast. The body of Christ is the people of God and not a crumb and a sip. The table of the Lord flourishes with life for all. To ignore the needs of the poor among you (when you possess the world's goods) is a contemptuous act towards both God and humanity. The unworthy participation in the body of Christ by wealthy separatists is the cause of both death and illness within the body. The neglect of the poor is the failure of the wealthy to judge their own behavior. Paul's letter is the Lord's judgment upon the wealthy for their neglect, their arrogance, their intolerable practice of separation.

Remembering the Lord is to fill the air around the table of *'koinonia'* not with chatter about everyday concerns, but rather theological discussion about the meaning of Jesus' life, death and resurrection. The educated (typically the wealthy) can teach the uneducated. Those with much can provide for those who need help. They can fulfill God's desire to love one's neighbor as oneself.

Remembering in light of John's Gospel

Remembering has the effect of bringing the 'quality of time' into a given moment in the present. Remembering the acts of God is a spiritual practice and functions through faith. A person can be feeling sad and lonely, but when a friend recounts to them a joyous moment, that memory turns their sorrow into joy. It is the qualitative element of time that enters the present. The contemplation of the meaning of Jesus' death on a cross is at the center of theological effort in relation to grasping the depth of God's love and understanding human reality.

We murder both God and humanity on a daily basis. We sacrifice to the political powers that wash their hands of responsibility. We promote the murder of hate in the name of religious dogma. We submit to the crowd and participate in the killing of the innocent through scapegoating mechanisms. We miss the meaning of the cross in relation to ourselves and in relation to the revelation of God's love made flesh, become a human being (forever).

To remember is to be a storyteller. I always remind my students, 'storytellers rule the world', either for good or bad. Remembering the acts of God is always good. Stories are easily remembered in contrast to philosophical dialectics or technical language. When we tell the stories of God we can be humbled at the truth that humanity kills the innocent, even God. We can be enraptured in love and hope at the story of Jesus' resurrection.

If we are to remember Jesus and remember the night the Lord healed the pain of Passover, we must look to the Gospel of John.[46] John's gospel does not record the communion ceremony. Rather, John's non-sacramental community replaces it with Jesus' practical act of washing Peter's feet. This act of humility, this willingness to love others as the revelation of God, requires that all of us become people of humility in relation to others.

The chiasm on the following page makes clear that Jesus' act of practical service was set forth as 'an example' for a given culture at a given time. It is notable that Jesus' washes the feet of Peter, the one who uses a sword, who will deny him. Peter is the one who Jesus is not sure of his love. Jesus washes the feet of the disciple who causes him the most grief. Jesus loves Peter.

---

[46] I reference the idea of the healing of Passover early on in this piece for affect. The Passover meal for Christians is replaced with the remembrance of the death of God's son during a love feast. In contrast God self-revelation displayed in the death of Egypt's firstborn for the freedom of Israel is replaced by a better sacrifice. God gives up his own son to death at the hands of humanity for the freedom of all humanity. Exodus 13:1-16 points to the death of the firstborn of Egypt as the decisive act for the deliverance of the Israelites and as the reason for the practice of Passover.

A Chiastic structure of John 13:1-19

Verse 1 "...Jesus knew that his hour had come..."
  Verse 2 And during supper when the devil had already put it into the heart of Judas Iscariot Simon's son, to betray him,
    Verse 3 Jesus, knowing that the Father had given all things into his hands, and that he had come from God and was going to God,
      Verse 4 rose from supper, laid aside his garments, and girded himself with a towel.
        Verse 5 Then he poured water into a basin, and began to wash the disciples' feet, ...
          Verse 6 "... and Peter said to him, 'Lord, do you wash my feet?'...
            Verse 7 Jesus answered him, "What I am doing you do not know now,...
              Verse 8 Peter said to him, "You shall never wash my feet."
                Verse 8 Jesus answered him, "If I do not wash you, you have no part in me."
                  Verse 9 Simon Peter said to him, "Lord, not my feet only but also my hands and my head!"
                    Verse 10 Jesus said to him, "He who has bathed does not need to wash, except for his feet,
                      Verse 10 "... but he is clean all over; and you are clean,..."
                        Verse 12 When he had washed their feet,
                          Verse 12 "Do you know what I have done to you?"

Verse 14 "If I then, your Lord and Teacher; and you are right, for so I am."

Verse 14 "...you also ought to wash one another's feet".

Verse 15 "For 1 have given you an example..."

Verse 16 "... a servant is not greater than his master; nor is he who is sent greater than he who sent him.

Verse 18 "I am not speaking *of* you all; I know whom I have chosen; it is that the scripture may be fulfilled, ' He who ate my bread has lifted his heel against me."

Verse 19 " I tell this now, before it takes place,. . ."

Remembering in Light of Passover

Passover occurs on the night that God is accredited with the death of all the firstborn. It is a night of blood placed at the entrance to the homes of all who would escape the death of their firstborn. In my reading of scripture, we are to understand that God is responsible for this pointedly specific act of selectively taking the life of the firstborn, of both man and livestock. It is this event that brings Pharaoh into submission and he releases the slaves to go with Moses.

The culminating lesson of the plagues temporarily breaks the will of the Pharaoh. Pharaoh will soon 'change his mind' because God in his mercy left Pharaoh with his chariots. This act of mercy was so Pharaoh's military force would stand as a deterrent to invaders. However, it is this culmination of the plagues that defines the problem of God acting in the world in relation to the social ills created by humanity.

God is put into a position where regardless of his mercy, patience, and educational acts, a human being like Pharaoh, who stands in the place of god, will not adhere to the voice of God.

It is because we refuse the voice of God – because we void our moral conscience through the pursuit of comfort – that we depend upon the exaltation of all types of messianic political figures. We produce Pharaoh. The rejection of God is always present in the temporal nature of human government. The state does not know and cannot know God. As a power, it falls at the feet of Jesus' cross. Pharaoh is a damaged soul who cannot let loose of his power, even to God. The ultimate power of the state is to take human life. This is what 'Pharaohs' understand; this is humanity at war with God. The result is the madness of war, the slaughter of the innocent; it is Pharaoh's chariots chasing God's people into the watery chaos of death. But God…

Killing the Firstborn

The killing of the firstborn is void of bloodshed (except for the sacrificial lambs), there is no pain or suffering, only a last breath. Yahweh is the Lord of life, not Pharaoh, not the state. Human beings kill, they shed blood; God does not.[47] In order to deliver the slaves from Egypt, God (Yahweh) has been forced to display his power over life

---

[47] When God provided the skins for clothing Adam and Eve there is no statement to say God killed any creature. Part of the function of Genesis 1-11 is to function etiologically and anthropologically on the human condition. The provision of skins for clothing reflects early human practice and rejects the comical effort to hide one's nakedness with leaves. The act of God to clothe Adam and Eve is revealing of a parental concern for Adam and Eve in spite of their failure to heed the voice of God.

in a manner that muddies his efforts to reveal himself as merciful love. The reason for the Passover remembrance meal is presented in Exodus 13:1-16. The verse below points to the death of the firstborn of Egypt as the reason to remember Passover. The death of the firstborn is the definitive act that breaks Pharaoh's will and results in the ensuing madness over the loss of his power. It is because Pharaoh threatened Moses life, a sign indicative of an escalation of violence and possible slaughter of the Israelites that God struck first.

> *Then Pharaoh said to him,*
> *"Get away from me!*
> *Take care that you do not see my face again,*
> *for on the day you see my face you shall die."*
> *(Exodus 7:28)*

In light of God's love for Egypt expressed in the refrain, "They shall know that I am Yahweh", it is evident that God is concerned about his self-revelation in relation to all humanity both powerful and powerless.[48] Nonetheless, God is on the side of the oppressed and contends with the oppressors.

> *You shall tell your child on that day,*
> *'It is because of what the LORD did for*
> *me when I came out of Egypt.'*
> *(Exodus 13:8)*

---

[48] Moses' is also concerned for God's self-revelation and the story is retold in Numbers 14:1-24. Moses pleads with God to forgive the Israelites in the wilderness. The wilderness generation who left out of Egypt was held responsible for the acts of God that they had seen, for those acts reveal God. The Exodus story is about God 'proving' and revealing God's self (without faith no amount of power can prove monotheism).

The story of God being prepared to destroy those who came out of Egypt (Exodus 32) is a picture of the need God has for prophets to speak and act on his behalf. Moses' argument for God to relent is not about the slaves, but about how God will appear in the eyes of the Egyptians.

> *Why should the Egyptians say, 'It was with evil intent that he brought them out to kill them in the mountains, and to consume them from the face of the earth'? Turn from your fierce wrath; change your mind and do not bring disaster on your people.*
> *(Exodus 32:12)*

It is imperative for the reader of scripture to understand, the Exodus story is the beginning of the revelation of God, following the stories of the patriarchs. The Exodus story is also comprehensive instruction on humanity in relation to God, the human condition, and the earth or natural world.

The killing of the firstborn is an act that God does not and will not repeat. This is particularly portrayed when we understand how the communion ceremony replaces and sits in contrast to the Passover. As Christianity spread, the love feast, the hospitality of table fellowship, became the celebration for the *koinonia* of the ecclesia. Paul's use of communion as a ceremony during the love feast in Corinth is initially about healing the hurt (even sickness and death) caused by social stratification. In relation to the Passover, the ceremony serves to replace the memory of the death of the firstborn in Egypt with the death of God on a cross.[49] The death of Jesus is the progressive

---

[49] In Christ, death as an experience is no longer foreign to God. Saying the cross displays the death of God is to communicate this fact; in Christ, God has experienced dying.

revelation of God that culminates in the resurrection of humanity. God will not allow death to have the final word.

The remembrance of the death of Jesus is to remember that when God came into the world and joined humanity, we collectively made him an innocent victim to our systems of power. In the Passover, masses of innocent firstborn lost their lives in order for God to use a people through whom he could reveal himself. Now the Passover is replaced by the humility of the communion ceremony, which is naturally set within a love feast marked by a celebration of fellowship and unity. The pain of God is revealed in the Passover ceremony. God did not want to participate in the killing of human beings over struggles for power, like the kings of the earth. The difficulty in getting a clear picture of God in the Old Testament is solved in the Lord Jesus Christ. God loves us to death, his death on a cross.

God does not desire to fight with humanity's relentless temptation to power through the state's need for a king or president. God is even concerned that states survive and flourish. On the other hand, God desires a people, a people who hear his voice and display the nonviolent God of love, as a body, an organism unified in the Spirit of Christ Jesus.

The Eucharist is a ceremonial tool for bringing people together. Its purpose is to unite believers of all ethnicities and social stratification in a way that the oppressive power of poverty is lifted. There shall be no poor among you is God's desire (Deuteronomy 15:4). Once people learn to live in a way that teaches and moves toward this end then the ceremony is no longer needed. The love feast is not divided; it is shared in a communal fellowship where the last are first, and the first act with the humility of a God who washes feet.

A Story of Two Worlds: Romancing the Bridge

The bridge from the U.S. base to Magsaysay drive in Olongapo looked like this when the story below took place.

I am an American, a child of the Western United States. My heritage is Irish, English, Indian and Jewish. My religious heritage dates back to the birthing of the Pentecostal movement in the U.S. When I was a child my parents made regular trips to take my sisters and me to Disney Land. I had gotten a work permit and social security card at twelve and I had kept a job throughout my teenage years. I washed dishes in a local restaurant, picked oranges and worked at an orchard ranch. As a teenager, I experienced the Jesus movement of the seventies and enjoyed the blooming of Christian contemporary music concerts at Knott's Berry Farm. I grew up never knowing hunger, always able to wear trendy clothes, enjoying the pool in our back yard.

She was poor; she grew up eating food discarded by children fortunate enough to have a packed lunch. Her heritage is Filipino. Her father, Porferio, fought alongside U.S. soldiers in World War II. She never had a new dress and her hunger had driven her to steal seed from a birdcage and taste coffee grounds. A bridge separated us. A bridge connected us.

The distance of seas and islands, continents and oceans, language, racism, nationalism, religion, and wealth (to name a few) all separate human beings. Bridges connect us; they make for ease of movement from one place to another. There are many types of bridges; some are made of steel, some of wood, some are wireless and make communication immediate, some fly across the skies, some bridges are more powerful, like love, family, and faith. I have spent my life romancing a bridge. It began when I lost my curly hippie locks to the electric razor of a USMC boot camp barber.

We had arrived in the Philippines aboard the U.S.S. Tripoli. I had heard stories of the beautiful Filipino girls that lived in Olongapo city and the wild life on the other side of the bridge. The bridge made passing over the river from the base to the town quick and easy. The wealth and power of the United States military sat on one side of the bridge, and the poverty of an exploited people on the other side. On one side there were U.S. housing developments, even mansions for high-ranking officers. There was a movie theater, a go-cart track; it was almost home. On the other side was lack, poverty, smell, pain, suffering, and death, on the U.S. military side was abundance, excess, power, and empire.

I crossed the bridge; the smell was overwhelming it was like standing over pools of water at a non-functioning sewer plant. The girls were there to meet us on the other side. Standing on the parapet of the bridge were young boys begging for change. Service men tossed coins into the pungent water and the boys dove in to fetch the pesos. The boys would rise from the water with the coin in their mouth to the drunken cheering of onlookers. Small canoes stabilized with bamboo outriggers and lit up with kerosene lanterns contained girls dressed like princesses; they too were there to beg for crumbs from the well-paid servicemen.

This was my second trip across the bridge. I had learned that the boys diving in the polluted water were sure to die within a short amount of time. I had seen the officers and gentlemen behave like deviants in town, and all my illusions of the moral greatness of America had vanished. I watched as drunken sailors laughed and tossed coins into the water and participated in the death of young boys. I had not yet become a practitioner of nonviolence. I was a young marine (trying to be a Christian). My anger over the treatment of the Filipino people, the complete disrespect for their wellbeing, for their women, for their children - it was more than I could hold in.

In a moment of adrenaline and anger, I blasted the first sailor across the head with a closed fist. It was a solid blow, rising from my feet through my shoulder. The sailor collapsed, his friend turned towards me and I kicked him hard enough to drop him to his knees. The next one looked frightened, as I was moving towards him with some uncontrolled rage. He turned to run but was drunk and slow. I slapped him in the back of the head. I decided to make a run for it because they were a group of about half a dozen. I ran to the end of the bridge, leaped over the side, called the boys over and gave them all the paper pesos I had in my wallet.

I would cross this bridge many times over the course of my life. It has become a symbolic power for me as it constantly reminds me of the power of bridges to connect and to maintain separation. Later, as a Christian, older, better instructed in my faith, I was at the bridge again. It was a hot day, very hot, one of those scorching days that offer no relief. A young mother with unkempt hair, exhausted, her clothes torn and unwashed, was sitting on the ground against a light post. Her baby was hanging loosely in her lap and unable to nurse, in the heat the baby was exhausted. Such sights are not uncommon in the Philippines; a person has to be careful not to let their heart grow hard. I walked over to the girl, knowing I could not save her from her life of hardship and suffering. I gave her a good amount of cash, equivalent to a month's wages for many Filipinos. I bent over and nudged her awake, she took the money and clenched it tightly in her hand. Still there was no smile; it was not enough. She needed more than I could give.

Years later I was at the bridge again. This time I was opposing the sex industry in the local towns and helping girls leave bar owners. There was an older Caucasian man that seemed out of place and interested in the children. To my delight I noticed a Filipino undercover policeman watching and taking pictures of the man's every move. The bridge was still maintaining the separation caused by wealth. The U.S. Military had turned over the base to the Philippine government and it was now an economic zone. The economic zone is home to numerous attractions, zoos, a 'SeaWorld', zip-lines and other activities, including a first-class marina. The Subic Bay Metropolitan Authority is the name of the former U.S. Military base. It also has a world-class mall and a toll road to connect both Angeles city and Manila to the former military base. The everyday Filipino must travel on a winding and often dangerous road.

Olongapo is still a town of bars, remarkably fewer than during the presence of the U.S. military. The music industry still thrives and Olongapo produces a number of musicians. A few years ago there was a small wharf and a walkway built along the river near the bridge. One particular evening, the mayor was holding a battle of the bands on the wharf. My son was with me and I arranged for him and his friends to play a number of songs.

They used the instruments that were available and played a set of songs that were definitively oriented towards Jesus, justice, faith and hope. I had come a long way from the day when I had attacked the sailors - a long way from a Marine to embracing nonviolence.

Although the bridge joined two different worlds, it still maintains a division, a separation between the powerful and the powerless. Yet, it really isn't the bridge that separates, it is the people who control the bridge, it is the powerful that determine who can pass over from lack to flourishing. Brave souls, loving souls challenge the power of bridges to separate. Humanity is divided; we remain segmented into the powerful and the powerless. There is only one way to cross a bridge and that is in love and peace. I met my wife on the poor side of the bridge.

Chapter II

Christian Institution or Christian Community

It is said that institutionalism is inevitable. To whatever degree this statement is true, it does not mandate surrender as the appropriate response. It is my preference in this piece to avoid long exposés on the failure of institutional Christianity through the centuries; this tragically disappointing fact is well known. We live in an age when the impotence of Christianity is portrayed before the eyes of the world. It is my conviction that we must return to the faith of Jesus, a faith that considered the entrance of God's Kingdom into the world to be inevitable.

The call of Christianity is not to produce a system for survival, nor is it to produce a system of power that ensures permanency as an institution in the world. The call of Christianity is to bring God into the world through our manner of living, to be the people of God. For this reason, how we live is more important than what we know in relation to the accumulation of knowledge. I say this with the endless production of academic journals in mind, each written with some claim to contributing to the grand field of knowledge in biblical studies or theology.[50]

---

[50] The absurd cost of Journals is evidence of a failed system of education that caters to the ongoing enclave of language possessed

Theology is the effort to communicate the disruptive power of truth and not reduce God-talk to explaining God's being rather than God's desire for humanity. God speaks, we hear and obey; our obedience is not slavish but lovingly adventurous, entering into the realms of peace where God abides. There is a living power of change so potent as to be able to alter the course of history; it is God ready to help Christianity in the world evolve toward visible manifestations of the reign of God in communal efforts that resist the tendency for institutional powers.

Christianity is not endogamous; it is ever reaching for the receptive entrance of God into the world through the people of God (the bride of Christ). The need for spiritual development of human beings is not fulfilled in dogma; rather it is fulfilled in the theological reflection of Jesus as Lord of the present. The pursuit of becoming a spiritual person cannot be accomplished through sacramentalism or attained through sheer discipline. It is a communal exercise, a commitment to collectively serving humanity in the name of Jesus.

Every good answer needs a better question. Every question needs new thoughts, fresh words, and a little color that turns ashes into beauty. Christianity cannot be reduced to humanism, but humanism is closer to Jesus than religious nonsense. We should bring a party every day to the sick, the lame, the dying, the poor, the oppressed, the prisoners

---

by a few, an enclave that is irrelevant to the masses of people involved in Christianity. The separation of the church from the academy is a real problem, the two should be co-dependent and this is not so for evangelicalism. Denominational schools also lack academic freedom based upon the encroachment of ecclesial institutionalism that is built upon divisive claims of authority.

and the addicted. Instead, religious people hide behind walls and speak about transcendence. They make sinners out of the righteous who share their food in desperation. Only a fool smiles all the time, or a clown, or a hypocrite, there is no best life on this side of the grave.

You cannot serve God without serving humanity. Institutional powers, grand buildings, replacing human presence with technology, raw power, all are inconsistent with the living, breathing movement of God in humanity. The Christian church is an exercise in giving up on all that constitutes how humanity is governed.

The manner in which the dress of the Roman Senate passed onto the clergy is indicative of failure. The politicizing of the faith, correlating the faith with the state, is the trespass of institutionalism (death) into the faith. If you want to be a Christian you have to jump into the muddiness of life and get dirty; robes, stained glass, and symbolic signs are all a distraction.

Institutional Christianity says you must live in the world (society's systems) and then attempts to offer you some religion on the weekend. So, church buildings sit empty most of the time. This emptiness is indicative of a disconnected institution. A community of believers should be concerned about all its participants and serve in job creation, entrepreneurial efforts, growing food (the miracle of multiplying) and educating their children. We have allowed the public powers to compartmentalize our lives and our faith.

Of course working with human beings is messy. However, if education is a communal value and everyone grows in the value of lifelong learning, then a lot of the mess can be avoided. Educating teachers to work in the Christian community is more important than pilgrimages to Israel, great choirs, television ministry, or the Sunday sermon. The establishing of communal values is an imperative and only the raw core of Christian faith is essential for communicating as dogma; e.g. the life, death, and resurrection of Jesus Christ as Lord.

Christian Communal Values

If Christian efforts for gathering believers worked with a minimal core of confession, then focused on Christian development through instructional values, the result would be healthier than the divisiveness of the present. Values must be biblically oriented spiritual ethics that move towards the goal of Christlikeness. I will provide a basic core of values and leave open the identification of values as communal exercise.

Key words for referencing these values is an important step for instructional purposes. To begin, conformation to the image of God in Christ is a process and can be referenced as 'Becoming'. Becoming is recognition of expected change in the behavior of a person as they grow in their faith.

Communal unity needs to be formed around sharing and not a pastor's vision for his ministry. Unity in a group of believers is not the eradication of individualism, but the fulfillment of the individual as an accepted part of the group. 'We are one' is an adequate way of communicating this value. Sharing is not individual ministry building, it is seeking to serve others in humility with grace, and the service is to meet practical needs.

Biblical literacy is an educational value that seeks to develop critical thinking skills for reading the biblical text. Biblical literacy involves an educational process that provides all community members with knowledge of the lenses, tools, and methods required for biblical interpretation. Biblical literacy is an imperative for the development of a healthy Christian community.

Identifying values built around scripturally based ethics for daily living, for meeting the challenges of living in a secular age, for reaching out to others, keep the Christian community active and vibrant. The three I have mentioned seem to be essential beginnings for value identification. I do not wish to produce a list because I think it is important for every Christian community to enter the spiritual journey of identifying life-giving values, for their particular place and calling in Christ and in the world.

Civil Law in Church and Community

We live in an age when the governing powers have limited our freedom to take care of ourselves by systemic licensing of services. Laws are also in place to protect people from abusive business practices. As a result, litigation is ever present in the daily affairs of a U.S. citizen. The teaching of Paul on absorbing suffering rather than going to court with another Christian is lost to the naming of a company, lost to the church as a corporation.

> *In fact, to have lawsuits at all with one another is already a defeat for you. Why not rather be wronged? Why not rather be defrauded? But you yourselves wrong and defraud — and believers at that.*
> *(1st Corinthians 6:7,8)*

In 1st Corinthians chapter six, Paul expects the Christian community to stay out of the courts. The ethical value of the community is not about who wins but about the reputation of Christ in the world. In a community where business endeavors belong to a member but serve the community at large, it is the power of money that separates and causes rifts in relationships. Paul instructs the Corinthians to resist the institutionalism that surrenders the autonomy of the Christian community to the secular authorities.

Relational conflict, in general, is often the cause for the exercise of power that excludes, scapegoats, and harms another believer. In such cases, the punitive power of authority excludes with established power structures and does not work at reconciliation or even at understanding. The victim of abuse in any type of Christian community or institution is a better person than those that expelled him/her and used civil law to do so.

The Entrepreneurial Community

The entrepreneurial community is interested in job creation for the flourishing of its entire people. This kind of ministry is desperately needed in our world. Church should be a place where everyone can find a job rather than just the few folks who are put on staff. A healthy Christian community works together to ensure the success of all its members in every good field of human endeavor. Job creation is a mission field waiting for the people of God to enter as ecclesia.

Investing in job creation provides a Christian community with an opportunity for bringing in economic resources that can enable them to care for the poor, the widow, and the orphan. Older church organizations and educational institutions thrive from the benefits of endowment funds, they are not dependent upon the people. The entrepreneurial community's response is job creation for the thriving of all.

I know that the inner working of a Christian community that participates in building businesses for profit so that those funds can be used by a non-profit religious group is complex; however, it can be done.[51]

---

[51] See: Redekop, Calvin W. *Mennonite Entrepreneurs: (Center Books in Anabaptist Studies)*, (Baltimore, MA: John Hopkins University Press, 1995).

CHAPTER III

Understanding Holiness

Understanding holiness is essential for avoiding the human tendency to attribute holiness to symbols, ceremonies, objects, places, or so-called sacraments. The worship of God is done in 'spirit and in truth' not in institutionalized religious practices.

I was once told by an old wise man, "It is God's nature to be holy; God cannot be other than who God is". His statement implicitly defines holiness as a word descriptive of the uniqueness of God as a being. Further, this statement suggests that God's nature is not to be equated with the idea of human nature. God alone is holy and attributing holiness to human beings is only so when their association with God is demonstrated in actions that bring God into the world. That is when we become temples not made with hands. If you want to build God a house then be a peacemaking child of God.

> *by which he has granted to us his precious and very great promises, that through these you may escape from the corruption that is in the world because of passion, and become partakers of the divine nature.*
> (2 Peter 1:4)

In contemplating the conceptual meaning of holy as a term descriptive of God's uniqueness and equating the term with God's nature requires a person to identify traits of God's person as revealed in the world. Initially, I think we must affirm that God is existence. There is no existence apart from God. No creature has life in itself, only God the creator. Existence, it is said, precedes essence; that God exists as a singularity as the 'one' God requires a word for expressing God's nature and that word is holiness.

> *And he is before all things, and by him all things consist.*
> *(Colossians 1:17)*

In Genesis 15 Abraham believes God's promises and his belief is equated with righteousness, yet Abraham seeks certainty, he requests or needs more than his own belief. God makes with Abraham a promise or covenant that is consecrated through a ceremony. In this covenant ceremony Abraham is instructed of Yahweh to bring three animals and lay them open, down the middle and two birds that are not cut into. The animals are placed in a drainage path forged by the rain, but the wadi is dry at the time of the ceremony. When the sun goes down a smoking pot and a flaming torch (representing the presence of God) pass down between the animals. This ceremony means the agreeing party will choose being laid open like the animals rather than fail to keep the covenanted promise. There exists in this ceremony an affirmation from God that God would desire disillusion of self if he did not keep his word.

After the ceremony, God tells Abraham, "Know this for certain..." God will give some tangible evidence that can produce certainty for Abraham; Sarah will have a son. Through the covenant ceremony, God has affirmed that his nature, his holiness, prohibits him from being anything other than who he is; God is holy, a promise making and keeping being. In due course God will provide humanity with a new covenant cut in his own flesh, a promise of love, grace, and life, culminating in resurrection. To be holy means to be responsible for all creation in such a way that creation can trust the words of the Holy one.

Abraham's promise is fulfilled and the encroaching powers of death in his wife's menopause are reversed. In time Sarah will give birth to Isaac. The certainty granted to Abraham is revealed in God's power over death, demonstrated through the gift of life from a dead womb. Death does not get the final word, for if the Holy one can reverse death in the living then he can bring the dead back to life. To be holy is to be Lord over death, to be the God of the living.

> *37 And the fact that the dead are raised Moses himself shown, in the story about the bush, where he speaks of the Lord as the God of Abraham, the God of Isaac, and the God of Jacob.*
> *38 Now he is God not of the dead, but of the living; for to him all of them are alive."*
> (Luke 20:37-38)

The holiness of God is revealed in God's love for creation. Love is a relational term that indicates a self-sacrificial willingness on the part of the lover to protect and provide for the beloved. God is culpable for the beloved's existence and therefore must teach the creature (humanity) how to live, how to exist in the world God has created. The Torah or law was understood to be instructional rather than merely legislative prohibition. In regulating wrong the Torah was instructive to the one with ears to hear.

> *Then Jesus said, "Father, forgive them; for*
> *they do not know what they are doing."*
> *(Luke 23:34)*

The great teacher has joined humanity through his incarnation in Jesus. The great teacher has experienced being human. Job once questioned God's ability to understand human experience.

> *Do you have eyes of flesh? Do you see as humans see?*
> *Are your days like the days of mortals,*
> *or your years like human years,*
> *(Job 10:4-5)*

God's culpability for creation, demonstrated in the incarnation, is indicative of God's holiness. God is not subject to the temptation of power; even omnipotent power. Holiness is more than omnific attributes. God can empty himself of omnific attributes and demonstrate who he is in a way that reveals holiness. This was made clear in the person of Jesus Christ. Humanity is not an experiment that God would change his mind about creating; humanity is to reflect the image, the holiness of God. God gains, even earns, the love of humanity by his acts that depict what it means to be holy. God joins the creation and makes being human a part of what it means to be God.

Humanity's first potential for living or being holy is found in the image of God that we bear. Next, is that we would receive God's gift of life declared through the good news of God's revelation through Israel, culminating in the life, death, and resurrection of Jesus and continuing through the birth of the church, the bride of Christ.

For a human being to be holy he/she must live out the image of God that they bear. They must be relational, redeeming, creative, promise-keeping people. Further, to be holy is to accept the suffering of the world and live under the rule of God who required a cross of his son, an act of love, a human response made by a human being to the will of God. So, we bless when cursed, we love our enemies, we pursue peace, we endure pain, betrayal, sickness and death while confessing the goodness of God our Father. We see a world to come where death is no more, and the sins of the past have all been healed as the Lord of Glory wipes away our tears.

Chapter IV

God Is

To say 'God Is' requires definitive claims with the purpose and intent of revealing. The Christian faith is accustomed to hearing 'God is love' or 'God is holy'. To say, 'God is', when speaking ontologically (of a living being) is to speak descriptively of the 'character' of God or of God's nature. To say God is wrathful, vengeful, angry is inconsistent with the revelation of God crucified in the Lord Jesus Christ. These thoughts belong to the manner in which human beings perceive God in relation to the presence of death and evil in the world.

The nature of monotheistic belief initially requires on the part of humanity a cry of culpability that holds God accountable for all human experience. However, God requires humanity to choose good, to develop ethically in concert with the moral conscience of a child, to experience the image of God in which they have been created and not to mar the image with despair.

God is not the creation, although through the creation we can begin to learn a little about God. Ultimately God must reveal God's self within the confines of human experience. God needs a story so that we can know God.

God is a Relational, Redeeming, Creator who keeps Covenant

After we accept and grasp the first two statements, 'God is holy' and 'God is love', then we are prepared to grow in our understanding of God, who is a relational redeeming creator who keeps covenant. God, who is love, who is holy, governs each term in this statement. I do not consider the statement exhaustive; however, it is weighted with truths about God that are revealed in God's story found in the scripture.

The Shema (Deut. 6:4) states that God is one. I believe in one God. I also think that attempts to understand the concept of the Trinity have some merit. I prefer to consider that this effort grew out of a need to understand the incarnation and the parakletos (Holy Spirit) in light of the New Testament revelation and story. To claim that God cannot become a human being is to limit God's ontology to our understanding and not recognize the omnipotent control of God over God's self.

God is Relational

God's self-revelation in Exodus 34:5-7 displays God's self-reflection as he passes before Moses, stating his name twice. Reflection upon one's self must be done in relation to both self and others. Self-reflection denotes that to exist and possess consciousness is to be relational. Within ourselves, as with God, our self relates itself to its self through self-reflection. We are social beings by created intent and this also denotes 'image' and 'likeness' with our creator.

We are dependent upon God to properly relate to others. We must draw upon his 'nature' or 'holiness' and receive all life as sacred in order to live in proper relation with others. Relational living does not consider people disposable, regardless of damaging ideas like labeling a person 'toxic'. This is so because God is redeeming and in his image and likeness, we also are to practice redeeming love.

I have chosen to begin this statement about God with the word 'relational' because before God redeems anyone or creates anything or makes any promises, God is relational. It is the Spirit of God who longs to unite humanity into a harmonious organism of relationally redeeming creative promise keeping.

Reading Psalm 133 in light of Redeeming Relationships

Psalm 133 teaches (this is clear if you read it in Hebrew) that when we can sit together and keep speech, working towards peace and resolution, then we bring the power of endless life into the world. I will offer some translation and an exegesis of this chapter because it is crucial that we understand how to live together in peace and work as agents of redemption in both human and divine relationship.

Psalm 133 teaches non-sacramental living. This is so because, as you will read below, the two metaphors sit in contrast to the 'possibility' and the 'blessing'. As metaphors, they communicate likeness, but they are not the human practice that brings heaven to earth.

The Psalm effectively unfolds by bracketing the religious metaphor and the aesthetic (nature) metaphor with the ethical practice that produces 'life forever'. In this sense, the Psalm teaches us that the ethical must govern both religious and aesthetic life. The ethical in the Psalm teaches us that to live in peaceful relationship with others is to live in relationship with the power of life, the life unto forever, the blessing that comes from God.

Grasping at the power of Eschatological Hope

> *How very good and pleasant it is*
> *when kindred live together in unity!*
> *It is like the precious oil on the head,*
> *running down upon the beard,*
> *on the beard of Aaron,*
> *running down over the collar of his robes.*
> *It is like the dew of Hermon,*
> *which falls on the mountains of Zion.*
> *For there the LORD ordained his blessing,*
> *life forevermore.*
> *(NRSV Psalm 133)*

Exploring the Relevance of one of Israel's Ancient Songs

In the gospel of John the phrase 'eternal life' is not limited to the future, but embraces the immediate.

> *Very truly, I tell you, anyone who hears my word and believes him who sent me has eternal life, and does not come under judgment, but has passed from death to life.*
> *(John 5:24)*

Interestingly, this concept of the presence of eternal life existing in the present as a power and/or reality is found in the Old Testament in Psalm 133. Likewise, the phrase 'Kingdom of Heaven' used in the New Testament is also understood to possess the now/not yet status given to the phrase 'eternal life'. According to the theology of the New Testament writers, we already possess eternal life and yet we wait for the consummation of this reality into the present. This now/not yet idea is not foreign to the Old Testament but is embodied in the 'hope pieces' found at the conclusion of prophetic judgment speeches. The power of eschatological hope is the bringing of the future into the present. Meaning, when we embrace the promises of the world transformed, we bring the power of transformation into the present.

Psalm 133 also presents the possibility for humanity to exist as a singularity, as found presented in the prayer of Jesus.

> *The glory that you have given me I have given them, so that they may be one, as we are one, I in them and you in me, that they may become completely one, so that the world may know that you have sent me and have loved them even as you have loved me.*
> (John 17:22-23)

So, Psalm 133 is rich with theological truth and reality that is utilized by both Jesus and the New Testament writers. To review, the specifics are: First, Psalm 133 presents the possibility for humanity to exist in 'unity'. Second, Psalm 133 presents eternal life as a reality that can be present in the now.

The parts of the Psalm need to be understood. The Psalm consists of four major parts. The first part is the first line, which presents 'the possibility'. The second part is the 'first metaphor'. The third part is the 'second metaphor'. The fourth part is the result of the actualizing of the possibility, (which is 'the blessing').

The Possibility

I will explain. The first line of Psalm 133 can be better understood by the English reader through the benefit of a more literal translation that adheres to the Hebrew word order. The first word of Psalm 133 is an exclamative, meaning the Psalm begins with a word that denotes emotion, joy, or even the equivalent of an enthusiastic 'yeah'.

> *Yeah! What good? What pleasantness?*
> *Sitting brothers as one.*
> *(Psalm 133:1)*

It is important that the reader realizes the Psalm is a transformative hope piece that is meant to help the reader move from 'spiritlessness' to 'Spirit'. The Psalm is meant to manifest the power of the eschatological hope into the 'now'. This is accomplished through the use of poetic language - language that uses idealistic memories of religious icons and the aesthetic dimension of nature to display the power of God.

The First Metaphor

In the first metaphor, oil is used as a symbol of the Spirit present in the anointing of Aaron, the first priest. This 'precious oil' flows down the beard of Aaron.[52] The reader is invited to imagine Aaron standing as a man of age filled with wisdom and anointed by God. His beard is the evidence of God's faithfulness found in the experience of the aged. As the oil flows further it begins to flow over the ephod worn by Aaron.

The ephod is an aesthetically pleasing object to view, it contains the names of the tribes of Israel carved into the stones attached to it. The reader finds the metaphor to reach beyond its symbolism and inspire the deepest feelings of the devotion. Now, the reader understands the brothers or 'brethren' to be Israel. Yet Israel is supposed to be a nation through whom all the nations find blessing, thus the metaphor has the power to make the reader understand that 'brethren' is synonymous for all of humanity.

The Second Metaphor

It is like the dew of Hermon, which falls on the mountains of Zion.
(Psalm 133:3a)

---

[52] A sacred vestment originally designed for the high priest (Ex 28:4 ff; 39:2 ff), and made "of gold, blue, and purple, and scarlet, and fine twined linen," held together by two shoulder-pieces and a skillfully woven band which served as a girdle for the ephod. On the shoulder pieces were two onyx stones on which were engraved the names of the twelve tribes of Israel. It is not known whether the ephod extended below the hips or only to the waist. Attached to the ephod by chains of pure gold was a breastplate containing twelve precious stones in four rows. Underneath the ephod was the blue robe of the ephod extending to the feet of the priest. The robe of the ephod was thus a garment comprising, in addition to the long robe proper, the ephod with its shoulder pieces and the breastplate of judgment. ISBE ed. By Bromiley BW 6

As the Psalm unfolds, the second metaphor extends the reader's activated imagination beyond the romantic memory of religious iconicity to the powers exhibited in the natural world. These natural powers are reminiscent of the theophanic appearances of God. Thunder, darkness, earthquakes, and a mountain in the Old Testament often accompany the presence and appearance of God.

Dew as a metaphor is used by the prophets and equated God's presence with the life exhibited in the faithfulness of the morning dew to freshen the earth. The blessing of God's life-giving presence that was exhibited in the natural world through the dew from Hermon upon the sacred place of Zion is expressive of the truth that God transcends the idea of a holy place. If you will, the holy place is reduced to mere symbolic significance for relating to and knowing God.

These two metaphors enable the reader to view the Psalm as a universal truth not bound by the structures of religious icon or symbol. The universal aspect of God's transcendent nature fulfills all covenantal promises through the power of the gift of life that comes from God. In this sense, Psalm 133 functions as a non-sacramental reality where the religious and natural world are used only as metaphors in light of the peace attained when people learn to sit together as one. It is notable that whenever a person is in disagreement with another and wants to assert their view, then that person will stand up rather than remain seated.

Both metaphors serve to build upon the actualizing of the possibility found in the first line. That possibility is humanity found sitting at the table of hospitality, pursuing peaceful resolution to all their conflicts. When people are capable of sitting together then there is hope for peace even amidst disagreement. Further, when people are sitting all together, or as 'one', then acceptance and understanding are present in their relationship. The idea of relationship is further established when the reader understands the word 'brothers' to be applied to all humanity. So, we might translate the first line again with some interpretive license:

> *Wow! Can you imagine the beauty and peace present when humanity learns to live as one!*
> *(Psalm 133:1)*

The Blessing

> *..... For there the LORD ordained his blessing, life forevermore.*
> *(Psalm 133:3b)*

> *My Translation: For it is there Yahweh commanded the blessing life unto forever.*

The final or fourth part of this eschatological hope takes us back to the first line. The locative word 'there' is identifying the action of humanity to sit as one (pursuing peace) and not referring back to Zion. The first line was the manifestation of all the good that the two metaphors could inspire. Now the first line is the object of the blessing commanded in the last line. Thus the blessing of 'eternal life' arises from human activity, an activity that belongs to all humanity and not just Israel. The universal aspect of all Old Testament hope pieces is found here in Psalm 133. The truth of the gospel is found in Psalm 133. The possibility for human beings to live at peace is not just an eschatological hope; it is also an effort to which we are to commit ourselves in relation to others. When we can sit together in understanding and peace we can experience the power of the blessing 'eternal life' in the now.

The need to learn to be peacemakers is part of the developmental process for the maturation of all believers. Jesus said

> *"Blessed are the peacemakers,*
> *for they will be called children of God.*
> *(Matthew 5:9)*

We live at a time when Christianity needs to be re-established as a faith that pursues peace and loves others (especially her enemies). Peacemaking is not the business of politicians and kings; their business is war, the expansion of their will and the good of their people over the good of other peoples.

It is the place of the church to speak for peace. Peace is achieved through understanding, through give-and-take, through acceptance of the other (and the other is always different). Peace is always purchased at a cost. Christianity is not the business of the state it is the person of Jesus alive in his people. Christianity cannot be enforced upon a culture or upon a people through the medium of governmental powers. Since the inception of the church, whenever the church is identified with the government then the faith of the church is reduced to violent expansionist activities. The voice of the church today should be a voice for the pursuit of peace.

In the book of Samuel one of the commanding Generals named Abner has some words that need to become our words.

> *25 The Benjaminites rallied around Abner and formed a single band; they took their stand on the top of a hill. 26 Then Abner called to Joab, "Is the sword to keep devouring forever? Do you not know that the end will be bitter? How long will it be before you order your people to turn from the pursuit of their kinsmen?" 27 Joab said, "As God lives, if you had not spoken, the people would have continued to pursue their kinsmen, not stopping until morning."*
> (2 Samuel 2:25-27)

We are brothers with all of humanity and yet we insist on the killing of one another as the solution to our problems. As long as we live by the sword we will perpetuate the power and response of the sword in the world. The industrial military complex will continue to devour our freedom and replace it with the power of the sword as the voice of America. The sword does not speak for God. We must remember that the word of God is more effective than the sword. We must pursue dialogue and understanding with all 'others'. We must learn to bring the power of eternal life into the present by sitting down at the table of the Lord. We must learn to universalize symbols and allow the power of the symbol to once again guide us to the God of all. We must partake of the flesh and blood of Christ by entering into his sufferings, by dying for the world through bringing a message of peace.

We create our own reality and sustain peace through covenantal agreements.

Creation and Covenant

Humanity participates in creation in two distinct ways. One is through the procreation of children; the other is through the creation of reality by making covenants that enable us to live together in peace. God of course, is the Creator, whose covenantal promises form the basis for God's self-revelation in history.

At the heart of the biblical covenant is the assurance of a promise sealed in a ceremony that symbolizes life with the presence of blood. This is so for Israel in circumcision; this is so for God through the cutting in half of animals and God's symbolic passing through the midst of the animals (Genesis 15:1-21). That God makes promises to humanity is of profound significance, for it is in the ongoing assurance of God's redeeming work and promises that humanity learns of God's love.

A covenantal promise is only as good as the character (word) of the person agreeing to the covenant. The covenant as a legal document is only as good as the legal system or the government that agrees to it. Our promises to one another should always be spoken with the assurance of all of our strength and being, and we lovingly work to support those promises. Love is always the unspoken assurance of all our relationships. Love is an unspoken covenant that dwells in us because God is love and we are his children.

When promises are written (covenant) they become a witness to our potential for being like God and keeping our word. A violation of a covenant can be addressed with the written document. Violating a (good) covenant is to resist the likeness of God we carry in our souls and court death's entrance into the world. How we keep our promises defines our person.

Jesus would teach us not to swear. God swears, and when he does, the oath given is unilateral and irrevocable. God has the power to fulfill his promises. We often find ourselves well-intentioned but unable to meet the desires contained in a promise. So, Jesus teaches us to be people of our word with simple statements of yes or no. For us human beings, swearing is beyond our capability for ensuring fulfillment. However, our word is not to be given lightly, for it reveals our character and gives witness to our faith and our God.

*A good covenant, a good promise, is always
a relational redeeming act of creation.*

Readings

In

Relational Theology

Part Three:

MALE-FEMALE RELATIONAL THEOLOGY

Introduction

Male-Female relational theology is an interpretive lens for reading scripture. The interpretive method most favorable for producing results is a canonical final form reading that exposes the narrative continuity of scripture. This approach brings to its service a number of interpretive tools, such as character development and literary structure, along with attention to subversive elements and normative defying characters. Subversive elements are often deconstructive of cultural norms and resist powers of dominance over others; this is so particularly in the case of the patriarchalism that oppresses women.

The theological concept behind the need to read scripture for developing male/female relational theology is rooted in the idea that men and women are created equal. This being said, the equality is, specifically, bearing the image of God. Further, this equality is not inhibited by the limits and particularity of gender.

That the image of God is borne in both male and female without variance implies that the image of God can only be fully revealed in humanity when men and women learn to live together without oppressing the image by inhibiting either gender from their right to contribute to the formation of family, culture, and society. The liberty given to the children of God has no room for domination.

The legitimacy of male-female relational theological readings is demonstrated by the abundance of scripture that comes to light when subjected to the lenses, methods, and tools of interpretation. My own study of the female characters of Judges is a remarkable example of the power of doing theology in this manner.[53] The narrative continuity displayed through the declension of the voice of the female characters in Judges is the phenomenal literary work of scribal genius, and divine inspiration shines as the underlying testimony to the self-authenticating power of scripture.

Male-Female relational theology is not purely feminist theology; rather, it is an effort to uncover the problems of male-female relationships in all life's expressions, and in doing so, be able to imagine another way of living together, free of erring and often normalized assumptions. The writing of theological statements produced through the effort of male-female relational theology is the guiding pedagogue for the development of said theology.

A quick example of theological and narrative continuity is found in the Cain and Abel story in relation to the silent

---

[53] See: Garner, Mike *Interpretive Adventures; Subversive Readings in a Missional School* (West Conshoshocken, PA: Infinity Publishing, 2015) chapter IV.

concubine of Judges 19-20. The motif of silence and murder (sacrifice) in both stories allows the reader to identify the silencing of women as a form of murder. Yes, the silent concubine was brutally murdered, but this is so because the voice of women was oppressed in society. Her own father would not listen to her and respect her decision to leave the violent abusive priest. The namelessness of the priest suggests that men lose their personal identity when their relationship with women in the world oppresses the image of God in the female.

The motif of personal identity is first revealed in the relational conflict and differences of Adam and Eve. Only after the failure of the first couple does Adam name his wife (Eve) and recognize her individuality. Prior to that moment, she is his 'flesh' and under his domination, for he is the one who has named all of creation.

The conviction of male-female relational theology is that when we learn to live out the image of God as male and female without any form of oppression, we unleash the God-likeness that unites us in the Spirit with our Creator, our heavenly Father. For this reason, the imperative for doing male-female relational theology is immediate.

Chapter I

The Human Condition

Created Equal

*So God created humankind in his image,
in the image of God he created them;
male and female he created them.*
Genesis 1:27

Regardless of one's views on the creation of humanity, whether immediate or evolutionary, the uniqueness of human beings is evident. The writer(s) of Genesis insisted that humanity's creation was special, set apart, and purposeful – an act of God's creativity unlike any other. This is demonstrated in the first creation account (Gen. 1:1- 2:4a) with some literary ingenuity through the use of the word 'create' (Heb: *bara*)

The word *bara* is placed seven times in the first creation account. The first literary device to note is the inclusio identified by the first and last lines of the initial Genesis creation account. In effect, the inclusio serves to insist that all of creation was the work of God (regardless of how it all actually happened). The Genesis creation accounts are theological responses to the existing myths of other nations.

The second use of the word create is in 1:21. Briefly, the specific use of the word applied to the sea monsters is a word play on the chaos motif; there are monsters in the watery deep. Within the context of creation, chaos exists, and this is the work of God. The potential for the eruption of chaos is acknowledged as a part of the good creation. The eruption of chaos will occur because of the reality forming human beings. The theology of the Hebrews is that God is greater than the chaos existent in creation. The story of salvation is a story that works from chaos to cosmos (order).

The first reference to ancient near eastern concepts of chaos is the presence of water. Ancient man held a primal fear concerning the vastness of the bodies of water that threatened their existence.[54] The waves of the ocean and the changing tides were for them a mystery. Water fell from the sky, surrounded the land-masses and yet was essential for life. So they personified water in their creation stories as a great dragon. In their philosophical meanderings on existence, water was present at the beginning and the entire cosmos was formed from the conquering and killing of the watery chaos dragon. The appearance of the dragon-like serpent in the garden is a picture of chaos. There is chaos in the garden of God and humanity is to take dominion over the chaos.

The next literary device of the word create is placed around the creation of humanity. In verses 26 and 27 of the first creation account, God uses the words create and image three times. The emphasis is clear, humanity's creation

---

[54] See Pritchard, James B. *Ancient Near Eastern Texts Relating to the Old Testament.* (3rd ed. Princeton: Princeton University Press, 1969).

is a distinct act of God to produce image-bearing beings. The word 'image' is introduced in verse 26 and the other two uses are in verse 27 where the word create is found three times. The words image and create appear in the following order, image, created, image, image, created, created. This is an interesting formation considering the previous use of inclusio. So the structure looks like this:

<u>Column</u>

    1   2   3

Image
Created
          Image
          Image
Created
Created

The male and female equally bear the image of God. It is the image of God that makes humanity distinctly different from all of creation. If you will, the thrice-repeated 'created/image' structure communicates in column 1 that the image is God's and God is responsible for the creation of God's image in humanity. Column two brackets column three as an inclusio, this insists that God creates both male and female. Adam's (unconscious) participation in the creation of the female in the second creation account is of no consequence in relation to the creation of the female and the sharing of the image of God; column three readily represents the male and female.

Learning to be Male and Female

The mythopoeic stories of Genesis 1-11 can be read as instructive for learning how we are to live together as male and female, equally created and equally bearing the image of God. The method for such an effort is similar to uncovering lessons for nonviolence when reading violent texts. The subversive element of the text that undermines sanctioned violence in violent texts can be applied to lessons on living correctly as equals, as male and female. The literary structure of Genesis 1:27 has refuted any superiority of Adam over Eve that might be derived from the second creation account.

It is important to understand that the minimalist presentation of scripture on such subjects (as we read in the first eleven chapters of Genesis) is the product of careful and purposeful thought by theologically and philosophically matured persons (scribes). In their world, writing is the work of only a few educated and paid elites. Obtaining the materials needed to write is immensely difficult, conservation occurs in both the preservation of documents and the art of brevity.

Genesis 1-11 is a reflection on the human condition in light of Israel's monotheism and cultural milieu. It is an etiology, a psychological reflection, a theological revelation, a masterpiece of literary work. It is the 'scripture' of both Jewish and Christian faiths. Within the confines of Israel's cultural world are the myths of the surrounding nations, the patriarchalism of their own culture and the limits of their own language and writing practices. Revelation, genius, and human limits mark the production of the creation stories; the word is always clothed in flesh. The creation stories are not explanatory history but theological revelation, written to serve God-seeking persons who understand that God always enters the human soul through the word.

Having said these things and in light of these thoughts, I will pursue teaching on how we are to live together as male and female. In Genesis 1, the human condition of the male and female is image-bearing equality. Genesis 2 and 3 begin to explore the human condition from the perspective of failure, from how things are. Yet, within these confines, there remains a subversive element.

The man (Adam) – an inexperienced life without a history or any memory to work with – is taught by God a prohibition that places limits upon his life in the garden of God. It is a single prohibition on a single tree and violating said prohibition leads to death. The tree of life is mentioned earlier by the narrator and sits in contrast to the fruit-bearing tree of prohibition that opens a path to acquiring knowledge beyond the structures of reality (evil). The portrayal of the man's actions speaks of the way things are; men control language and (more specifically) 'naming'.

The absurdity that the man would find a suitable helper among the animals is at least laughable. The story is setting up the presence of the female gendered, image-bearing human as a gift. The Lord brings the woman to the man. The man speaks; it is a poetic piece of proclamation. He recognizes the woman as being like him. As the man named the animals, so he names the woman. Her naming, however, is not a personal name; it is a gendered naming of another human being. The writer is leading us to his counter-cultural teaching that announces the male-female relationship as superior to all others. Why is this so? In their culture, the female left her father and mother, but in the foundational text, the male leaves his family to cleave to his wife. It is the man who needs a helper, a female who brings qualities into the human experience that correct the man's tendencies to power (e.g. naming).

Naming is a significant act in the scripture and in the culture in which it was composed. The next few chapters consistently ignore the naming of women except for instructive moments (as I will demonstrate later). It is also important to note that the woman was created as 'help' and not reproducing partner. This lifts the concept of the woman as a 'creature' above her capacity to bear children; her existence as a thinking, living human being is equal to the male.

It is important that the reader remembers the purpose of the story is to teach us about the human condition, challenge the reader to be more, and respond to the competing stories of the Ancient Near East. All of this takes place within the context of Israel's monotheism. Within the teachings these stories offer, we find ways to move closer to God, closer to the one who has barred our entrance into the garden of life with a flaming sword.

In the absence of God, the woman seeks to explore the new reality she has entered. Her inward conversation with a wild beast (a serpent) is reflective of the human capacity to hear the voice of God in contrast to the power of the human intellect that questions the limits God has placed on our reality. If we are to experience the life that comes from God, the life represented as being resident in a tree, then our freedom requires choice. God has given them all the trees except one, so much to learn, so much to explore, but the image-bearing woman seeks understanding that is barred by a prohibition. She is but one-half of humanity; the man is with her at the tree. The scene is instructive; the man is failing to remove the serpent (the wild creature) from the garden of life. Eve is also guilty of being enamored by this creature's presence to the degree that her inner dialogue is depicted as proceeding from the serpent.

The serpent can represent the chaos motif or the dragon. Likewise, the serpent is a sign of Egyptian power, which is meaningful in light of the time in which the Genesis stories would have begun forming. The fruit (innately powerless) represents a prohibition given by God. The serpent represents the power of domination over creation. The woman has experienced the dominating power of naming yielded by the man. The man views Eve as property (flesh of my flesh, bone of my bones) rather than gift and helper. Men think of women as property. Women seek to be equals.

Of course, the man is present at the tree with the woman and is as interested as the woman to reach beyond the limits of creation, beyond the underlying structures of reality in order to gain power in the absence of God. Rather than finding God within the confines of life where so much good is present, humanity – male and female – seeks knowledge at the expense of one another, at the expense of the other. If the man lets her eat, what will happen? If he eats, what will happen? Neither stops the other from violating the prohibition and eating the fruit.

To take dominion over the creation is to do so within the confines of the voice of God that calls humanity back into the garden of life. To desire, to respond to the voice of power, the voice of the serpent of the Egyptian system of governing is to eat fruit that leads to death.[55]

The failure of male and female to live together equally is seen in the counter-cultural instruction of the narrator that men leave father and mother, rather than the woman doing so. It is a call for men to respond with a corrective to the way women are treated as property by males, whether their father or husband.

The failure of male and female to live together equally is seen in the silence of the man when the woman is thinking (via her inner dialogue with the serpent). The lack of equality in their relationship (produced by Adam's naming of Eve) needed Adam to speak with her at this crucial moment. When the woman eats and does not die, the man joined Eve and ate of the fruit. The man was willing to sacrifice 'half' of humanity in order to learn the outcome of eating this forbidden fruit.

The writers artfully portray the thought of the woman, as her thoughts flow through the spheres of human existence; the aesthetic, the ethical and the religious.

> *So when the woman saw that the tree was good for food,*
> *and that it was a delight to the eyes,*
> *and that the tree was to be desired to make one wise,*
> *she took of its fruit and ate;*
> *and she also gave some to her husband, who was with her,*
> *and he ate.*
> *Genesis 3:6*

---

[55] The Egyptian Pharaoh's head-dress bore the images of a vulture and serpent. The vulture represented the power of Pharaoh to take life and the serpent represented wisdom.

First, the woman makes an ethical decision: the tree is good for food. Second is her aesthetic observation: the fruit is appealing to the eyes. Third is the religious sphere: the woman desires wisdom. Her violation of the prohibition is consummated in her power to act.

The woman's power to reason is affirmed by this piece of inner thought. The silence of the man suggests the intimidation felt by men who view women as property when women demonstrate intelligence. It is important to note that both the male and female eat the fruit; the will of each, violate the prohibition and does not adhere to the voice of God that walks with them in the garden.

Upon eating the fruit, the primordial couple recognizes their nakedness. Shame enters reality with the effort to be more than creatures. They are not the 'seed' of God, they are creatures, and their godlikeness is limited to a yet unlearned image. They cannot become like God outside the confines of their own creatureliness. Their life is dependent upon obedience to this voice that walks with them in their mythic garden.

Adam blames God and the woman, the woman blames the serpent, God curses the serpent and the ground. Outside the garden an environment hostile to the naked human beings must be overcome; Spirit and flesh must learn to live together.

Pain and Desire

The ensuing response to the disobedience of the man and woman is a sad commentary on the daily reality faced by humanity. The man is told that the ground will not produce for him and he will have to toil in order to live.

That he listened to the voice of his wife is not license to justify silencing women or blaming women for the human condition brought about (in the story) by the disobedient act of eating of the fruit from the forbidden tree. Rather, it is appropriate to note the individual culpability applied to the man. Although they are in the words of Adam, 'one flesh', they are separate persons. Adam's failure in relation to Eve is he did not speak with her in a helpful manner but left her alone with her thoughts. This theme of individuality is affirmed by the naming of the woman, which takes place after the fall. It is the ability of the woman to act independently that sparks the need for Adam to recognize her individuality.

> *The man named his wife Eve, because she was the mother of all living.*
> *Genesis 3:20*

The man's attitude towards the woman is expressed in the poem of exclamation spoken upon God's bringing her to him. The Hebrew language does not employ the word 'one'; the woman is yet unknown to the man, although he has named her with a gendered term (woman). Adam has not recognized the individual agency of the woman, nor considered his own individuality in relation to the woman.

> *Then the man said,*
> *"This at last is bone of my bones and flesh of my flesh; this one shall be called Woman, for out of Man this one was taken."*
> *Genesis 2:23*

The man must face a hostile world and endure the sweat and toil of labor. The woman will experience pain in childbirth. The work of the man will separate him from his wife and her child-bearing pain will separate her from him. The difference in gender and the need for relational understanding is solidified in the human condition outside the garden. The disruption of disobedience has solidified a give- and-take relationship. The woman was 'taken' out of the man, but the man is now to take from the ground in order to care for the sustenance of the woman and their offspring.

The woman who took the fruit from the forbidden tree to share with her husband will share her body with the man and with the children she will birth. Her misplaced desire will now be directed towards the continuance of life through the giving of herself to her husband, in spite of the pain of childbirth. The individuality and otherness of the male and female are established in their relation to how each sustains life. The man labors to bring life from the ground and the woman labors to bring life from her body.

The pain of the woman bonds her to her children in the hostile world outside of the Garden of God. The man is from the ground and is dependent upon his relationship to the ground for life and dependent upon the woman for the continuance of humanity in the face of a world where death is the result of their disobedience to the voice of God. The independence of the man and of the woman to act in ways that pursue exploring their existence beyond the structured reality of life created and ordered by God is halted by the hostility of life.

The hostile presence of pain, of suffering, of the death that is in their world, is all indicative of their inability to live in relationship with God, the underlying structures of reality (the world), and one another. So begins the story of redemption, of reconciliation, of learning to live.

Adam must learn to speak with his wife as an equal, as one upon whom he is dependent. Eve must learn to engage the man in conversation and not wander off in her thoughts. The woman is prone to anxiety because she is a sensuous creature who feels deeply and experiences emotions with a physical engagement that surpasses the man's. She is a giver and the man is a taker.

The female capacity to imagine and romanticize is set in contrast to the man who takes, names, and seeks to rule over the hostile world through his toil. The man rules over the woman's sensuousness; she is dependent upon him in order to birth children. Within these structured realities the male and female must learn to live as equals, created in the image of God. If they do not learn to live together in a mutual relationship of love and equality, if they do not teach their children, violence will prevail. The challenge set before the man is to speak with and teach his wife of all that he experiences and learns; the challenge of the wife is to listen (rather than dream) and speak with the man.

Sex and Violence are Inseparable

Wherever violence is present we find the failure of men and women to live together as equals. The 'one flesh' and 'lack of shame' in Genesis 2:24-25 denotes equality and intimacy. In this piece, the man is held as the primary person responsible for ensuring the success of the 'marriage' relationship. Verse 25 clarifies that in such a case sexuality (nakedness) is sanctified. The becoming one flesh is the mutual relationship of life (not mere copulation).

> *Therefore a man leaves his father and his mother*
> *and clings to his wife,*
> *and they become one flesh.*
> *²⁵ And the man and his wife were both naked, and were*
> *not ashamed.*
> *Genesis 2:24-25*

This verse is counter-cultural and challenges the accepted norms of Hebrew society in which the female leaves her family to join the male's family. The reading of this verse requires that we acknowledge it is reaching from a later time back into the primordial world of beginnings. This enables us to read verse 25 as a statement applicable to the garden and to the present. It also allows the use of narrative continuity as a method for interpreting; meaning we can read with knowledge of the entire biblical story.

It is the exposure of all that one is to another in the marriage relationship that is represented by nakedness. The female does not keep hidden thoughts and the male overcomes hiding by speaking rather than silence. So much for the strong silent type. Learning to live with others begins in the model set forth by father and mother. Perhaps we can say Adam and Eve failed to do this in light of the Cain and Abel story. If we can learn to live together as male and female we can produce a healthier world, and ideally end violence. God will be present and work to help us if we seek to achieve such growth as relational people.

Religion Violence and Polygamy

> ²³ Lamech said to his wives:
> "Adah and Zillah, hear my voice;
> you wives of Lamech, listen to what I say
> I have killed a man for wounding me, a young man for striking me.
> ²⁴ If Cain is avenged sevenfold,
> truly Lamech seventy-sevenfold."
> (Gen 4:23-24 NRS)

Lamech is the first practicing polygamist in scripture; he is the archetypal representative for males who practice polygamy. His words set in a poetic piece display the artistically condensed truth the writer wants to communicate to the reader. The biblical writers expected us to enjoy the adventure of thinking when they wrote.

The names of Lamech's wives are taken from Hebrew words meaning, *ornament* and *shadow*. Adah is an ornament, she is the beautiful wife and Zillah is left to live in the shadow of Adah. The fulfillment of the marriage relationship portrayed in Genesis 2:24 is impossible, one wife is an ornament and the other reduced to shadow; one is favored, one is hidden,

Lamech's killing of a young man for some trivial assault reflects the birth of male machismo in relation to women. The poem delivers a subtle threat to his wives: he is capable of murderous violence over a small matter. Further, the poem suggests that his behavior is approved of by God, who forgave Cain and protected him.

Lamech suggests that taking life in an act of vengeance for a small matter is an act that God will bless. Lamech's theology is void of mercy and utilizes errant religious claims in order to justify his act and require subservience from his wives.

Polygamy is an act of violence against women and is justified by the misuse of religious belief.

The Threat of Chaos

Genesis six begins with a mythical story that serves to acquaint the reader with the condition of humanity at the time of a great flood. The flood itself is a "mabul," a disruption of the cosmos in response to the violence that has filled the earth through the practices of the 'sons of God' the 'Nephilim'.[56] The monotheism of Israel requires that God be held accountable for the flood. The flood story is composed in response to other flood stories written throughout the ancient near east. Ancient man's fear of the primeval waters, of the great oceans, of the power of water to erode the earth, of evidence observed in fossilized sea creatures, all contribute to the compilation of flood stories.

Utilizing narrative continuity I understand the 'sons of God' to identify the oldest men on earth who are few living amongst a population of younger human beings. The 'sons of God' are also 'Nephilim', or their direct descendants are the Nephilim. They are 'like' Giants in the eyes of the younger population. They take women freely, possibly seeking to breed their seed continually into humanity as a form of eugenics. This abuse of women and human sexuality is at the root of the violence that brings the flood.

---

[56] The Hebrew word 'Mabul' is used only for referencing the chaotic flood of Noah.

CHAPTER II

The Liberation of Women as Theological Enterprise

"The 'naming' of males as the authentic image of humanity

has corrupted theology and oppressed females

through both classic theological readings

and historically through socio-cultural politics."

Mike Garner –

Male / Female relational theology is directly related to liberation theology because both seek to identify the socio-cultural, political, and theological structures that oppress a portion of humanity; in this case, the female. The practice of liberation theology is to begin with a preferential option for the poor. In Mujerista, or womanist theology, the preferential option is, in particular, the female who is subject to structures that inhibit her humanity. The basic concept is that the liberation of the poor allows for the healing of the wealthy, who are oppressors. In male / female relational theology the same is so: a preferential option for women that liberates their humanity (their voice and body) has the potential to heal society and liberate the oppressor from their sins.

The Relationship of Liberation Theology and Latina Readings of Scripture

Mujerista readings for liberating Latin American women is part of 'la lucha', the struggle. The 'la cotidiana' daily struggle is to identify the oppressive structures of the Latin American woman's daily experience and read the bible through the lens of texts that liberate.[57]

In concert with Iganacio Ellacuria's concept of spiritual intelligence beginning with facing reality, the Latin American Mujerista seeks to understand herself and identify the oppressive socio-cultural, political, psychological, and religious ideologies that inhibit their right to participate equally in life. The goal of Mujerista readings is peace and justice for the mujeres of Latin America.

The mujerista utilizes her 'moral imagination' to construct a world where Latin American women function equally in the public sphere and regain the loss of their freedom to oppressive structures and determine their lives as full participants.

The mujerista theologian reads the scripture from a moral perspective and rejects texts that subject women to oppression. Mujerista readings are driven by experience, not merely personal experience, but the experience of the 'cotidiana' that is lived out in relation to others, particularly ethnic and gender experiences as a group identifies the mujerista's world.

---

[57] See: Ed. Alejandro F. Botto and Pablo R. Andinach, The Bible and the Hermeneutics of Liberation. Atlanta, GA. SBL, 2009. Pg. 181

Mujerista theologians focus on the texts that speak of the contribution of women in the Bible. This practice is to give attention to the female characters of the bible and how those characters promote life amidst their particularized struggle; 'lucha'.

The Latina practicing mujerista readings practices male / female relational theology and recognizes the subjectivity of their experience in relation to others. Meaning, the liberation of the Latina is dependent upon the liberation of the male also, in both positive and negative aspects. The mujerista practices a communal theology beginning with women and expanding into the larger community of family, church, and society.

Of particular interest to Latin American women is the reading of scripture immediately applicable to their experience. The day laborers parable (Matthew 20:1-16) is applicable in both their homeland and their immigrant experience in the U.S.

This brief introduction to the liberation theology of Latin American women is to demonstrate that male / female relational theology is always liberative and always radical in a world that legitimizes a reality of oppression as normative. The only acceptable reality for liberation theology and male / female relational theology is the 'reign of God'. Moving society towards the reign of God is a step towards liberation and is to be celebrated, but the struggle endures until 'thy kingdom come'.

The Women of Jesus' Birth and Resurrection

Jesus' mother is a canonized saint of inviolable status and reputation. This is not so with all the women Jesus' encounters in the gospels. Mary Magdalene epitomizes the female presence in the life of Jesus. This divide between Jesus' mother and the other female characters in the gospels begins with the lineage of Jesus where Tamar, Rahab, Ruth, and the wife of Uriah sit in contrast to Mary. Perhaps Mary's youthful experience coupled with the presence of Jesus throughout her life keeps her free from the experience of the other women in Jesus' life?

Jesus' birth marks a new beginning for humanity; the incarnation of the word in flesh provides the ultimate model for human achievement. Jesus' resurrection marks another new beginning: the first person to rise from death to life without end. The initial witness to be surprisingly greeted by the resurrected Lord is Mary Magdalene. The reputation of Jesus' mother was protected by her husband Joseph, whereas Mary Magdalene is without a male to defend her reputation (heart) and Jesus' takes on that position.[58] We need not focus on the names of the women, but on their character and role in the life of Jesus.

In the longer ending of Mark and in the gospel of John, Jesus appears to Mary Magdalene and sends her to tell his 'male' disciples that he is alive. The prominent female character to give witness to the resurrection of Jesus is Mary Magdalene. In the time of Jesus, women were not accepted as witnesses; a teaching derived from the Torah and built upon the absence of women as witnesses in matters of law and because their oaths could not stand if their husband or father so chose. That Jesus chose to have a woman, specifically the woman Mary Magdalene to be his first resurrection witness and sent her to his

---

[58] We need not focus on the names of the women, but on their character and role in the life of Jesus.

male disciples is intensely meaningful. It is interesting to note that Augustine referred to Mary Magdalene as the Apostle to the Apostles.

The framing of Jesus' life by Mary his mother and by Mary Magdalene his follower extraordinaire is significant. The witness of 'mother' Mary is contained in a song. The witness of Mary Magdalene, the 'loose' woman, is delivered to the male disciples of Jesus. The disciples (excluding John) scattered, but these two women were present when Jesus was on the cross. Mary Magdalene with the 'other' Mary accompanied and aided Joseph of Arimathea to the burial of Jesus. Mary Magdalene (unlike the disciples) could not let go of Jesus even in his death. It was Pilate who ordered guards to be placed at Jesus' tomb to forestall any rumors of resurrection. We are not told, but it is within reason to think that Mary Magdalene and the other Mary held to a hope unseen, so they went to Jesus' tomb.

That Jesus makes his first resurrection appearance to Mary Magdalene speaks of Jesus' faith in, care for, and understanding of, a woman subjected to the oppressive powers of male domination. That this woman is commissioned to speak to the unbelieving disciples testifies to the way of God in the world. God speaks through, works with and honors oppressed women who follow him. Women begin life in innocence like Jesus' mother, without men caring for their reputations they experience abuse and suffer 'demonic' oppression (that is, disarray of the soul) but upon meeting Jesus they become reliable witnesses and commissioned spokespersons for the gospel of God. In a world of male domination, Jesus liberates women from the perceptions of males and mercifully delivers them from the pain of their daily struggle.

Promises and a Beautiful Heroine

Genesis twelve records the calling of Abraham, the recipient of promised blessing. The second half of the chapter is about Abraham's efforts at self- preservation and the extraordinary woman who is his wife. It is an interesting way to introduce the father and mother of Israel. In Abraham's world the practice of endogamy is normal and being married to your half sister is not offensive. In contrast to the disjunctive beginning of marriage relationships in Genesis 1-11, the marriage of Abraham is marked by a wife whose companionship and navigation of life with her husband is truly admirable.

At sixty-five years of age, Sarai joins Abraham in an adventure initiated by Abraham's spirituality - an encounter with a God who makes him a promise. However, a drought and the survival instinct of Abraham caused him to move away from the land to which God had called him. It is at this point, we learn the name of Abram's wife and the degree of love she has for her husband.

Sarai is a beautiful woman in spite of her years. How she maintained her beauty is likely to be as important to Pharaoh as the fact that she is in appearance a model for standards of beauty. The maintenance of a woman's physical appearance as she ages is a trait and a skill to be passed on to younger women. That Sarai has not given birth to any children also contributes to her youthful appearance. Sarai is blessed because she is beautiful and married to Abram. In spite of the rigors of life with Abram, she has been able to preserve her beauty.

Abram is convinced that her beauty is a problem that will threaten his life if they are to live in Egypt where beautiful women are gathered up for the god-kings harem. Abram asks Sarai to only say that she is his sister if the Egyptians come to add her to Pharaoh's house. The trickster motif appears in this passage as a survival technique when one is in the weaker or powerless position.[59]

We are not told how Sarai felt about Abram's request for her to subject herself as a sacrifice for Abram's survival; all we know is that She complies. After all, both she and Abram are powerless; the blessing of physical beauty has become a life-threatening problem. I suspect this older couple has found happiness just being together. They could have used other means to bring children into their life if they had so desired. Sarai's love for Abraham is demonstrated by her courage to preserve both of their lives in the event her beauty subjects them to the whims of a god-king.

The text does not offer us any indication that Sarai was left untouched during her stay in Pharaoh's harem.[60] It does appear in the text that Abram received 'payment'

---

[59] Israel's stories preserve an admirable respect for practices and behavior consistent with the literary character of 'the trickster'; this is particularly so when their ancestors were in a position of weakness in relation to the person whom they deceive. Powerless persons have always used 'Trickster' wisdom. The Tales of Uncle Remus are a modern example of colorful yet subversive stories that reveal how African American slaves used deception and wisdom to live in an environment extremely hostile to their well being.

[60] Although the similar episode in Genesis 20 insists that God kept Abimelech from touching Sarah, in Egypt, Abraham and Sarai had not yet received the promise of a child from Sarai's body within a year's time. Further at sixty-five menopause has surely passed and Sarai cannot bear children when she is in Egypt.

for Sarai's presence in Pharaoh's house. I suspect Sarai's skills for maintaining beauty increases the value of her presence with Pharaoh's concubines.

How Pharaoh learned that the plagues were a result of Sarai's presence is not divulged to the reader. Perhaps Sarai informed him of her status as the wife of a man who received promises from God? Regardless, the heroic self-sacrifice of Sarai to risk her sexuality to save Abram is a harsh account of life's challenges in the life of Abraham and Sarah. It is possible from the text to conclude that Abram did not consider Sarai to be essential for the fulfillment of God's promise. While such an attitude is viable in light of these events, it is one that will need to change.

The reversal of death in the body of Sarah is an important theme for the Abraham narratives. Sarah must grow into the promises of God as much as Abraham. The story of Sarah is inseparable from the story of Abraham. God will clarify that Sarah is the one who will birth the promised son, and Sarah is the one who will experience the reversal of menopause in her body. Through the reversal of menopause, she will experience a form of resurrection power in her person. The problem of sterility does not lie with Abraham as we see in the Hagar story. He appears to be quite virile with the slave girl Hagar and continues to be so with Keturah and other concubines after the death of Sarah.

Only if we acknowledge the influence of culture, of patriarchalism, and read carefully with attention to the female characters are we able to appreciate the Abraham narrative as the Abraham and Sarah narratives.

The Growing Faith of Sarai

Abraham is not alone is his journey or in God's promises. Sarai is not to be excluded from the blessings promised to Abraham As his wife, they are her promises too. It is apparent that until God spoke to Abram and made promises of offspring that Sarai's barrenness was not a problem. Prior to God's entering their life, this well-adjusted older couple lived together without any apparent conflict; they were content with one another. Because of the promise(s) Sarai experiences the pain of her barrenness.

Abraham has lost Lot as a family member capable of carrying on the family culture. Their individual wealth has separated them and Lot's character is revealed to be less than Abraham's. Abraham has been out seeking God and experiencing moments of divine encounter. Sarai can only assume that it is the Lord who has kept her from bearing a child. Her claim affirms her faith in the Lord's ability to open her womb. On the other hand, her impatience and desperation cause her to take matters into her own hand.

Abram was willing to sacrifice Sarai's sexuality to Pharaoh, in order to preserve his life. In the end, it turned out well for him: he acquired a healthy amount of wealth and God returned Sarai. Perhaps this alone should have awakened in the old couple that the promise was not exclusive to Sarai.

Abram was not told to go to Egypt, nor is Sarai told to offer the body of her young slave girl to her husband in order to fulfill the Lord's promise. Perhaps Sarai's experience as a sexual sacrifice and her love for her husband hardens her heart and makes the sexual sacrifice of a younger female merely an unfortunate part of the broken reality of life. She has not learned that the Lord is able to reverse the effects of death in her body.

Hagar, the Egyptian girl, is likely part of the 'wealth' Abram acquired after his time in Egypt where Sarai lived with Pharaoh. Sarai's complicity in the abuse of a young woman is the marked sign of an abused woman or of a woman whose wealth and pride block her from considering the person of Hagar. Perhaps Sarai's failure to become pregnant in the house of Pharaoh, a lack of understanding about male infertility, and the culturally accepted practice of surrogacy or concubinage all prompt Sarai to abuse Hagar.

The Interpersonal Dynamics of Disordered Male/Female Relationships in Society

The social normalizing of disordered male / female relationships releases forces that affect the best of us. We cannot live in a world of social and cultural norms that are contrary to living out the image of God as male and female and remain untouched or unaffected.

For example, the power of thought in the A.N.E. provided the male with the power to reproduce and reduced the woman to an incubator. This ideology placed the male in the position of life-giver and made the woman a receptacle, a necessary but impotent vehicle in the reproduction process. This kind of thinking about human reproduction exalts the male and allows for the practice of polygamy and concubinage.

I think we can detect the effects of this belief in the relationship of Abram and Sarai. Since women are merely incubators, then Hagar can be used and the end result is a son for Abram. However, as the story unfolds and Sarah is promised a child, Sarah's natural bond to her son results in the rejection of Ishmael and Hagar.

This might explain Abram's willingness to go along with Sarah's plan to use Hagar. Abraham is identified as the one who will be the father of nations. Sarai is not immediately identified in the thought of Abram as the woman who is essential for the fulfillment of the promise. However, for God, Sarai was always the one through whom God intended to fulfill the promise to Abram.

The problem with God's activity of self-revelation is the times of absence when God's presence becomes elusive, so Abram and Sarai act according to the way the world is; rather than the way the world could be. Sarah's abuse of Hagar is directly related to her own status as a 'broken incubator'.

Rahab

Heroine Archetype Exemplar

Myth and Conquest Narratives

As a genre of literature the book of Joshua is a conquest narrative. Conquest narratives are political histories written to justify the displacement and killing of people groups that once occupied land, which is now in control of another people. Conquest narratives are history from the perspective of the powerful. It is common for this particular genre to incorporate religious belief. The book of Joshua is structurally composed to expose the conquest narrative's assumptions of righteousness or justification.

Joshua 1:1-9 is the narrator's perception of Joshua's understanding of the direction of the Lord for his actions as the leader of Israel after the death of Moses. The speech in its entirety is comprised of established theological promises and claims found in the preceding books. Like all conquest narratives, the origin of memorials is part of the book of Joshua, so some stones are placed at the Jordan to commemorate the crossing (Joshua ch. 4). The miraculous sign at the Jordan is to validate the work of the Lord to 'drive out' the inhabitants of the land (Joshua 3:10). The appearance of the messenger of Yahweh and the declaration that he is on neither side is deconstructive of textual claims about God's commands.

The story of Rahab challenges the accepted norms for Israelite identity because Rahab and her family are accepted into the fabric of Israelite society. The story of Achan signifies the loss of Israelite identity by failing to adhere to the values of Israelite society by violating the laws of destruction (kherem).

The treaty with the Gibeonites portrays Israel's acceptance of 'trickster' wisdom as admirable (Joshua 9-10). Likewise, the Israelites honor oaths agreed to, even though the weaker party was not entirely honest. Agreeing to live as servants to Israel in peace is consistent with the rules of war in Deuteronomy ch. 20.

The sons of Anak in chapter 15 bring the 'mythical' into the text of Joshua. The incorporation of myth into the story is a literary device to communicate that the text of Joshua is both history and myth. A conquest narrative by nature is a tool for indoctrinating a nation's people into the historical 'myth' of their superiority and right to live as rulers over people that were in the land before them; exaggeration of the conquest is common to this genre.

Rahab

In the eyes of her family, Rahab is a heroine who saves them from being slaughtered by the Israelites. As an archetype, Rahab is cast as a model for the inclusion of the most unqualified outsider. James, the brother of Jesus, places Rahab alongside Abraham as an exemplar for accomplishing the works of faith that constitute righteousness (James 2:25).

In the book of Matthew, Rahab is listed in the genealogy of Jesus as the mother of Boaz. Boaz receives the Moabite woman Ruth as a wife in accordance with the kinsman redeemer legislation of Leviticus 27. Ruth is the great-grandmother of David. It is apparent that the inclusion of Tamar, Rahab, Ruth and 'the wife of Uriah' in the lineage of Matthew's gospel speaks of the redemption of gentile women whose sexuality did not limit their role as mothers in Israel.[61] Hosea's God speech in 4:14 makes men responsible for the sexuality of women and is consistent with the lack of any condemnation for the sexual exploits of these women.[62] This is so for all

---

[61] It is likely that Tamar is also a gentile (Canaanite) because Judah was taking wives from people who were not Israelite.

[62] I will not punish your daughters when they play the whore, nor your daughters-in-law when they commit adultery; for the men themselves go aside with whores, and sacrifice with temple prostitutes; thus a people without understanding comes to ruin. Hosea 4:14

except Bathsheba whose name is not used in the lineage. I think Matthew understood Bathsheba's actions to be intentional from the beginning when she lit her bathing area to seduce David.[63] She was a married woman and did not suffer any oppressive realities comparable to Tamar, Rahab, or Ruth.

In the conquest narrative of Joshua, Rahab as a character is set in relation to Achan. As Tamar was more righteous than Judah, so Rahab is more righteous than Achan. Achan's lineage is recited back to Judah. Rahab is a woman of questionable character and the quintessential Canaanite. Rahab is subject to destruction; Achan is an insider and not subject to the destruction. Rahab is a loose woman; Achan is an unbelieving Israelite.

Rahab is an archetype for all gentiles exempt from Kherem and accepted into Israel; Rahab believes! She is a prostitute, a Canaanite, a traitor to her people in her efforts to live out her faith in the God of Israel. She believes the Exodus narrative and affirms the Israelite conquest as unavoidable and so she seeks peace. She is wise in her actions and her personal treaty-making.

In the book of Hebrews, Rahab receives Israelite spies in peace and receives peace. In the book of James, her works of faith are set forth as a model to all gentiles, even as Abraham's is for all Hebrews.

---

[63] Bathsheba is noted as the 'wife of Uriah' and this draws the attention of the informed reader to David's murder of Uriah. Jesus the messiah is not like David.

A Story: Guardians of Life

Calapandayan down the road from Barrio Barretto is a Dangerous Place for Anyone

The Abuse of Women and the Unraveling of the Social Fabric

The systemic abuse of young women in the Philippines finds its roots in the expansionist powers of empire, that empire being the United States. I recall arriving in Subic Bay aboard the USS Tripoli in the seventies. At that time, the sex industry was flourishing and the clientele were young military men. Thousands of girls lined Magsaysay Drive and Rizal Avenue in Olongapo City. All were poor and looking to marry an American. Today the US military has left, but the industry that flourished under the complicit eye of US officials has not shut down.

International sex tourism is a growing trend across the cities of Subic, Angeles, Cebu, Manila and other 'tourist' destinations like Palawaan and Boracay Islands. A number of bar operators are retired military men that have become little more than pimps and molesters. The Australians have also made their contribution to this group of maladjusted men.

The clients of the young women are now (mostly) old men seeking some "macho" image of enduring virility amidst their failing health and impotency. They have no future to offer these young girls and their inability to govern themselves speaks to their mental illness. Morally, they lack the fiber to see past their false sense of self as the macho male amidst the over-sexed Polynesian woman. This unfortunate and damaging stereotype of the Asian or Polynesian woman contributes to the illusion that the girls actually like them.

If I could take you with me to enter into the darkness that is the life of young women in the Philippine sex industry, you would find girls that, in many ways, are no different than the ones that line the halls of high schools and colleges in other parts of the world. Yet, their lives are very different. Very few girls are fortunate enough to marry a foreigner that will love them and aid them in the transition from a traumatic past of abuse and lies to become healthy functioning human beings. Usually, these girls have at least two children within five years (often four). Some of them contract STDs that endanger their health, also AIDS is a growing concern in the Philippines. I know of a number of young women sent home from the sex bars to the province to die of AIDS.

Most of these girls are 'recruited' from the poorer areas of the Philippines. The recruiters allure them with the promise of legitimate employment and paid boat fare to the supposed location of their new job. However, when they arrive they are locked in a room, often chained, stripped nude and raped–unless their virginity is intact, for then they can be sold. Through a process of building fear, humiliation, and false claims of indebtedness, the girls become pliant victims ready to be managed by a mamasan (an older woman who manages younger ones in the industry). In the areas where sex tourism abounds, signs for a Mamasan with her own stable of girls line the streets. Business for the sex mafia is booming.

The business of selling Filipina women (girls) requires organized deception and abuse. First, there are recruiters that work for the men that dehumanize the girls and prepare them for the mamasan. These men ensure a constant supply of women to the bars that line the streets of sex tourism areas. The bar owners are dependent upon this system to supply them with the women that are used and discarded at an increasing rate, due to the cost paid in the soul and psyche of these young women. The final person to 'purchase' the Filipina does so under the guise of a 'bar fine.' Although prostitution is illegal in the Philippines, this system is not regulated, for its simple rewording of the bordello jargon. A 'bar fine' is paid to the bar and the girl is allowed to leave with the customer. Girls are not given any choice; they go with whomever they are fined. It is not uncommon for bar owners to have their own rooms or small motels adjacent to their bars. The money from the bar fine is usually divided between the bar and the girl. Often the girl receives nothing due to the bar manager's claim that the bar is not making any money.

These girls live in constant fear of the bar owner or manager or Mamasan. Often when we have gotten the girls away from the bars for a meeting, the owner or manager would show up at the place where we were meeting. The girls are the property and livelihood of these persons that prey upon the weaker sex. The mind of these girls is a complex maze of culture and abuse.

The damaged psyche of the female personality is a result of the constant abuse experienced by the girls that work in the bars. As the guardians of life, women naturally tend towards kindness and self-sacrifice. When these attributes of the feminine personality are damaged by the abusive life experiences of a bar girl, she suffers disorientation and lapses back and forth from gentleness and weakness to deception and anger. The female's contradictory behavior is perceived by the male predator as mental deficiency due to lack of education and not understood to be the effects of the male's abuse. The male desires the feminine attributes of kindness and nurturing. They typically tolerate the deception and anger as a 'defect' in the female, which justifies the abusive activity of the male.

Women are the mothers, daughters and life-bearing members of every society. When law and the moral obligation of society do not protect them, then that society is guilty of the sins that the women commit as victims. In the Philippines women are for sale.

We entered one of the most dangerous areas and one of the most dangerous bars. Our purpose was to rescue a girl from the imprisonment of the bar. At the last moment her fear would not allow her to cooperate with our plan and we were unable to secure her freedom. During our effort a girl came off the stage completely nude. My wife smiled at her and said, 'hello sweetheart' and spoke to her in Tagalog. My wife embraced the nude girl; she threw on some strings for covering and sat down by us to talk. We purchased a very expensive Sprite to 'pay' for her time. Within a few moments she was weeping profusely and I and my wife longed for some way to be able to help her. The best we could do was offer to pay her way back home or help her to be placed into the PREDA Foundation home for women.[64]

---

[64] PREDA is the People's Recovery Empowerment and Development Assistance located in Subic Bay. Father Shay Cullen founded the PREDA foundation in 1974. Shay is a Columban priest and missionary from Ireland.

Chapter III

A Story: Meeting Grandpa Pinyon

Porferio Valenzuela Tibe was my father-in-law. He passed away in 2006 one day before we arrived in Tacloban. My first time to meet him was in 1976 while obtaining a birth certificate for my wife (his daughter). We flew to Leyte and traveled to La Paz where her family lived and where she was born. Over the years I learned to appreciate and love this man whose life was marked by a gentle spirit, kindness and love for others. I share this story with a smile and thankfulness for "Itay" (Philipino for Father).

It was 1976; I was a young Marine planning to marry a Filipina girl. She needed a birth certificate in order for us to fulfill the requirements to receive marriage approval from the U.S. officials. Her grandmother had called her Nympha, but her name given by her parents is Trinidad. Nympha and I made our trip to La Paz on the Island of Leyte over a weekend.

I was stationed at Cubi Pt. part of the Subic Bay military base. Traveling to another Island was prohibited without express permission from your commanding officer. There was a sign at the end of Magsaysay Rd. in Olongapo that forbade U.S. personnel from traveling beyond that point. I had travelled beyond it many times helping a street vendor named Joseph Laxamana, who sold Puka-shell necklaces. My friend Abraham and I had provided Joseph with enough monies to build a Nipa home for his family, and Joseph had taken me on tours through the sugar cane factory and the outlying areas.

We left on a Friday afternoon for Manila and caught a flight to Tacloban City Leyte. The road to Manila was mostly dirt, the bus was without air conditioning and the windows were stuck in whatever position they happened to be in. On the way through Pampanga the bus would pull over and allow food vendors to board and sell their items to passengers. After a mile or three they would be let off the bus at a spot where they could board buses headed the other direction and make their way back home.

The roads had lots of potholes, the trip was dusty and the weather was typically hot. One of the persons that would board the bus along this section of road was a club-footed boy of about twelve years. He would sing acapella; I was always amazed at his delightfully powerful voice and range of vocal skills. As he walked the aisle of the bus singing, passengers would place coins in his hand. He would of course move slowly and need to brace himself with his hand on the seats as he moved down the aisle.

The Victory liner Cubao bus terminal in Manila is, to this day, a busy and vibrant place of organized confusion for the first time traveler. We had only a single bag and quickly stepped out into the road to catch a taxi for the domestic airport. Nympha had never been on a plane; her reaction was quite different from mine. My first flight was in a Cobra attack helicopter when I was a mechanic in training. The pilot told me to take the stick and my brief effort over the beach area of Oceanside, California was a lot of fun. However, Nympha initially amazed at how homes and the landscape appeared so small, had a minor panic attack. She cried out, "Mike" and pulled on my hair with her eyes looking really big.

In Tacloban we spent the night with Nympha's sister, Norma, who sold mangoes at the market place near the straight between Leyte and Samar. I insisted on my need for a shower and was directed down a dark lightless space a couple of feet wide between the market fronts. There was a bucket and a hose bib and some boards to stand on. I stripped down and began washing myself only to be disturbed by a large pig kept on the other side of a piece of corrugated sheet metal. I thought, well that explains the smell. I managed to finish my shower and to keep my clothes off the ground, there was no place to hang or set them. When I finished showering I was able to step back into the light all-fresh.

In the morning I stood in the road and looked out at the city; I believed God would one day have me return to share my faith and produce a church. I still have that picture in my mind of the early morning empty-street and vacant market place, a place normally bustling with activity. After a quick breakfast of fish and rice, we went to the local bus loop where the brightly colored jeeps and a few vans were adorned with the local saint (Santo Niño) and assorted slogans of faith. On the front windshield the vehicles had crude little hand painted signs with their destination. We took a small van with plywood seats; the driver packed the van with people and a number of men rode on the luggage rack along with their goods they had bought in the city and were taking back home; everything from fighting cocks to clothing, lanterns and food items.

Nympha and I had sent a telegram to her father, informing him of our planned arrival and our need to acquire a legal copy of her birth certificate. This moment in life was all a wonderful adventure for me (much like most of life). The raw beauty of the Philippines was not yet touched by the ominous presence of concrete. Wood and bamboo houses with Nipa roofs were still the primary building materials for most homes.

As we pulled into the village of La Paz there were a number of persons awaiting family members and loved ones next to a Nipa covered bamboo bench. Among them I saw a tall Filipino man whose appearance stood out from all the other persons. He wore a cone-shaped rattan hat and boasted a healthy Fu-Manchu moustache. Strapped to his side was a traditional two-foot long bolo knife. Nympha smiled, touched my side with her elbow and said, "Dat's my dad".

Porferio greeted me with a captivating smile and handshake. He spoke English with the flair of a poet and the vocabulary of an educated person. He was a charismatic soul with a charm that gripped everyone in his presence. After meeting the family, Itay and I went to the Catholic Church to view the baptismal records. The church was open and there was no one in the building. Casually, Porferio walked to the back of the church and opened the office doors to a room containing numerous books. The books were logs of baptismal records that affirmed dates of birth.

Itay knew which book to pull from the shelf; it was a typical lined journal book about nine by twelve. The births were listed by year and month. First, Itay shared with me the birth of one of his children who died at a month old. His living children were three older daughters followed by four sons. Then we located Trinidad Remandaban Tibe, born June 4th 1955 to Porferio Valenzuela Tibe and Luciana Remandaban Tibe.

After affirming her birth and age, we walked on this crisp Saturday over to the city hall. No one was working but the door was open. Itay said to me, "No worries, I have worked here in the past. I know how to make a certified birth certificate". Itay typed up a record of birth on an official document, placed a stamp on the document and pressed it with the seal of the registrar for the city La Paz. We had the rest of the day and a portion of Sunday morning to enjoy before Nympha and I would begin our trip back to Olongapo.

When we opened the doors to leave the city hall, news had spread: a white man was in La Paz. I was told the only other white man to visit La Paz since World War II had been Pat Sayre, a member of the Navy who married Nympha's sister. So, when Itay and I stepped outside there were over a hundred kids wanting to touch my skin and look at my blue eyes. They followed us around for several hours until all of them had gotten to check me out up close.

We arrived back at the house where Nympha had been sitting and talking with her mother and other women about her faith in Jesus. I would sleep for the first time on a bamboo bed when the night came. First, however, Itay had plans to enjoy the afternoon. He told me that I was like Marco Polo making traveling great distances to foreign lands. He shared with me his experiences of fighting alongside U.S. soldiers during the liberation of Leyte. Porferio had been hired by the U.S. military to guide them throughout the island and root out Japanese troops.

We sat on wooden bench at a table outside a Sari Sari store; Itay on one side and I on the other. He insisted I taste the local drink 'tuba'. The tuba made from white sap of the palm tree was the reddish variety, colored with the bark of the Lauan tree. I explained that I practiced abstinence from alcohol consumption. Itay insisted that since I had traveled such great distances, since I was going to marry his daughter and in light of the possibility that he would not see her again, I must drink with him because he was a 'drinking man'.

I'm not sure I gave much resistance; eating balute and dried fish required some sort of strong redeeming chaser! So Itay filled my rather large cup with tuba. I took a sip and the tuba needed a chaser it was not a palate pleaser; Itay recommended a little coca cola. We sat and ate, as time passed I consumed my tuba and Itay watched to ensure my glass never emptied.

In the midst of stories about life as a Filipino, Itay shared with me his militaristic version of the Lord's Prayer: "Our father who art in the states, building great battle ships to fight in the Pacific, great be thy name, thy ships come, thy will be done in the Philippines as in the United States. Give us this day troops to fight and plenty of ammunition, so that we may overcome our enemies, and lead us not into defeat but destroy our enemies. For thine is the power, the might that rules the world."

As a young man from a small town I had been struggling with the apparent power of the American empire. The behavior of the U.S. military around Subic Bay I found despicable and inconsistent with all I had ever been told about the honor of the U.S. and her efforts in the world. Itay's inversion of the Lord's Prayer was both comical, and tragic. I laughed with him, but through my intoxicated state I knew I would never forget this moment and this prayer.

I was sitting on a bench like any picnic table bench and if you slide to far near the end without other persons holding down the bench, well it will topple and you will fall on the ground. I laughed so hard with Itay that I had slid to the end of the bench and fell on the ground. A little later we began making our way back to the family home.

La Paz was without streetlights; candles and little bottles with some kerosene and a wick provided light for people in their homes. It was very dark; we had been sitting, talking and laughing until late. The clouds darkened the night, blocking the light of the moon and the stars. Itay and I were walking with our arms around one another and singing the Philippine national anthem that he was teaching me line by line. The entire town was silent and the candles and lanterns distinguished, it was late. The animals were howling back at Itay and I as we sang together. Then he said, "Ah Oh", it was Nympha and her mother (Inay). They had come to retrieve the drinking buddies that were disturbing the whole town with our singing.

Porferio Valenzuela Tibe is the tall man second from the left. This is a picture of his baptism at Leyte Beach. He was baptized in 1984 during the time my family and I lived and worked in Tacloban City. Itay continued to seek God throughout the rest of his life. He cherished a picture Bible left behind by my daughter. The family still had the Bible in 2008.

Over the years I grew to understand and love this man, Porferio. In the following years I would witness his kindness and generosity and learn to understand the subsistence ethic required of the poor. For years, each month I sent Porferio a check for support of the family and to buy birthday and Christmas gifts. When I arrived to visit in 1982, the family had moved to a Barangay in Tacloban. My brother in-laws and I built an extension onto the home. During our building project, I spoke with the neighbors and learned that each month Itay shared the small gift I sent the family by purchasing food for others in the little area of Sagkahan. Itay and I communicated by airmail for many years. His poetic eloquence shined in everything he wrote as did his patience and love for his family. Porferio lived a typical Filipino life at a very different time than I had witnessed. I will see him again.

The Subsistence Ethic of the Poor

Subsistence ethics is the accepted manner of living within an environment of life threatening poverty. It is important to understand the complexity of an ethical life under the crushing power of oppressive poverty. The person accustomed to subsistence as life's reality does not view the world like a person free from worries over shelter, food, clothing, water, healthcare and education. Rather than thinking of the poor as possessing a mentality of poverty based upon their responses to life, it is important to understand the subsistence culture as an ethical culture.

The ethical culture of subsistence communities is a culture of sharing and at times desperation. The poor are dependent upon one another; the one who has more than they need for the day can keep other community members free from the suffering of lack, whether the need is small amounts of money or food or clothing. The daily hope of the poor is to have enough to meet the needs and demands of the day. They do not have the luxury of planning ahead.

Experiencing the Subsistence Ethic

A Story

My father-in-law lived in a small barangay on the edge of a city. The people all knew one another and lived within feet of each other. Their small Nipa homes provided very little privacy and were primarily for sleeping, changing clothes and cooking. I had built an addition on his existing structure and attempted to remodel the rest during a visit. Over the years we provided my father in-law (Porferio) a monthly international money order. At times I would send him a little more for various reasons, such as purchasing a bike for one of his grandkids or to buy a pedi-cab so his sons could work and provide an income for the family.

He would not buy a new bike; rather, he would spend a fraction of the amount sent him on an old rusty bike with a wooden seat and no rubber on the pedals. He simply never spent the extra funds to purchase a pedi-cab (a three wheel bike with a cart to provide a ride for passengers). However, when I would arrive a couple of years later to visit I would learn of his generosity to support the families in the community with his 'windfall'. His subsistence ethic judged the needs of the people near him to be of greater importance than new bicycles or investments like a pedi-cab. My frustrations with my father-in-laws failure to spend the money as I had wanted were quickly silenced by the stories of those he blessed.

Subsistence Ethics and Endangered Guardians

Women subjected to oppressive social structures do not choose to become prostitutes. In such cases, these women make an ethical decision based upon subsistence ethics to alleviate the threat of death in oppressive poverty and sacrifice their sexual purity, in order to save their family. Most poor women (girls) do not make this decision freely. They are often initially victimized by sex traffickers or drawn in by the presence of a sister already working and sending home life-saving monetary support.

Although these women (girls) suffer outsider status in relation to their family and community members, they also experience a sense of nobility for their sacrifice. This knowledge of their role as saviors to family members provides them with a sense of dignity in the midst of an experience where dignity is lost to the depravity of male abuse. The endangered guardian compartmentalizes her experience. As a sex worker she is working from the position of an oppressed victim who has sustained a conscious choice in order to save her family. As a human being she is better than the males who dominate her working world. I have heard every endangered guardian I've ever spoken with declare her righteousness (or justification) as care for her family, often sending a younger sibling to school so that she or he might be free from the grips of poverty.

The essence of the law in scripture is 'preservation of life'. The legal demands of the law can be set aside in order to save life. The women (girls) subjected to social structures of poverty, lack of education, and the needs of family reach a point when they, their family and their culture, view sex work as a legitimate activity within the experience of a subsistence ethic for sustaining life. In Thailand, a poor family will rejoice over the birth of a female child because she can help the family endure the horrific reality of poverty. It is not that the poor do not know how to think or are inflicted with a poverty mentality. Rather, it is we the privileged who have not experienced their world; it is we who do not understand.

It is not that we should legalize sex work because we recognize the grace given to endangered guardians. Rather, we must dismantle social structures that cause human beings to live under an ethic of subsistence. We must also dismantle the systemic abuse of women and girls by punishing those that profit from their dilemma. This is particularly so in Asia, where the presence of the sex industry was birthed by American, Japanese, British, French and Dutch colonialism through the presence of military forces rewarded by their own governments with (sexually) conquering the (women) colonized.

The Poor as Examples of the Kingdom of God

The poor learn to share in order to survive. Their ethic of subsistence recognizes the co-dependent needs of one another. Out of their own need they provide for one another so that life may continue. They discover their security in sharing, in caring for the well being of one another. Further, the suffering of the poor enables them to recognize the contempt for life and God expressed in the ever-acquiring 'rights' of the wealthy.

The scriptural view on women like Tamar, Rahab and Ruth all demonstrate an ethic of life practiced by women otherwise viewed by society as 'loose'. Abram flees the drought in the land that God called him to and becomes a refugee in Egypt. Abram prepared Sarai for the possibility that she would be taken for her beauty and asks her to save his life. Sarai's captivity in Pharaoh's herem is profitable for Abram. In the initial captivity of Sarai we are not told that she was not violated or abused; it is expected that she would be.

War and famine are causes of mass migration. Refugees of war and famine are subject to poverty and trafficking of the women for the sexual pleasure of the landed. The men suffer the indignity of not being able to provide for their family through the exploitation of their strength. If we understand Abram to be the father of faith then we can understand Sarai to be the mother of the people of faith. Our mother was a trafficked refugee in the land of empire.

A Story on Teaching the Rich and the Poor

These are homes outside the wall of the Lapu-Lapu dumpsite where the people who occupy these homes work each day in the smoldering refuse and tropical heat in order to survive.

The Children of Lazarus from Kenya to Cebu

In 2004 I made a trip to Embu, Kenya with my son and some young people. My son and I were teaching the Kenyan's regularly during our stay in Embu. I taught the story of Lazarus and the Rich Man to a group of pastors and leaders. Although they spoke English, their Pastor, Elias, aided me as an interpreter. I spoke slowly and utilized a white board and emphasized my points by using colored markers. The events of that day form the following story.

Jesus is a storyteller. This particular story of the Rich man and Lazarus is a creative invention, a fictitious story. As a story, it has a specific universal purpose and touches on cultural norms experienced by Jesus' audience. A good storyteller introduces the major characters at the outset of their story. As the characters are introduced, certain aspects of their role and behavior are immediately revealed through naming, appearance, status, dress, and their first words.

The naming of a character is an important literary device for the storyteller. The lack of naming can also be important. As Jesus begins his story, he introduces the major characters. The first character is a rich man. The rich man's name is not given throughout the entire story. The rich man lives a life of opulence; his clothing is likened to a king's (the color purple denoted royalty in Jesus' time). His undergarments are possibly silk; his food is prepared to delight the palate, and he lacks for nothing.

As the next major character of the story is introduced, we learn that the rich Man lives in a world where others can be excluded by the presence of a gate. The rich man lives in a 'gated' world that separates him from the outside. At the gate of the rich man's life lies a poor man. Initially, the poor man is not named. At this point in the story the rich man represents all rich men and the poor man represents all poor men. However, the next line names the poor man. His name is Lazarus. Lazarus is an Aramaic form for the Hebrew name Eleazar, which means 'God helps'.

The story of the Rich Man and Lazarus is a story of humanity's division; it is a story of the powerful and the powerless. The poor man, Lazarus, full of sores is immobile and must fight off the wild dogs roaming the streets of first-century Palestine. While the rich man is satisfied with the finest food prepared, food made to be aesthetically pleasing to the eye and tasteful to the palate, the poor man longs for crumbs that are consumed by the rich man's pet dogs. Crumbs are for dogs, but outside of the rich man's gate there are no crumbs, nor are the dogs pets. Wild dogs seek to consume Lazarus, tauntingly licking at his sores.

The story is contrasting the differences between the way the two segments of humanity experience "life under the sun". The powerful lack for nothing; the poor die. Lazarus dies. We are not told that anyone came to gather up the body of Lazarus and place him in a pauper's grave. We have been told about wild dogs that lick at his sores. The rich man dies and is buried. The poor man died and was carried to Abraham's bosom. The absence of a burial for Lazarus leaves the reader with a picture of a frail, defenseless body, now prey for wild dogs.

In Jewish writings, the bosom of Abraham, (the man of hospitality, who prepared food for the LORD and his messengers), is a way of speaking about a place of honor at the divine table of God. God has finally helped Lazarus, the man whose name means 'God helps'. God gave Lazarus rest in the bosom of Abraham. God's messengers lifted Lazarus up to a place of honor in the bosom of the patriarch, Abraham, the father of all Israel, the father of faith, and in that sense the father of us all (Galatians 3:7, 29).

The rich man is given a burial, no doubt a celebration and eulogy matching the wealth he acquired in his years upon the earth. However, there is a problem the poor man who was laid at the gate of the life of the rich man is with Abraham while the rich man is in Hades. The reader is to understand that this story is a theological fiction for purposes of teaching. Jesus is teaching about role reversals, about the powerful and the powerless, about injustice in social stratification. As the story proceeds to the underworld it takes on mythical proportions. Jesus' moral teaching is greater than any supposed communication on actual events of the afterlife.

I continued to teach the Kenyan's the meaning and teachings of the rest of the story. I discussed with them the absurdity of the rich man in flames, thinking Lazarus could bring relief with a drop of water, or that the rich man could identify Abraham. The rich man has a family and wants to secure a better end for them. However, he excluded from his circle of care a man named Lazarus. Abraham comforts Lazarus. Lazarus has finally received help. He belonged to the family of Abraham, to the family of God. The rich man is excluded, separated, and suffering.

Why didn't God help Lazarus when he was alive? The Lord had provided help: there was a man who had acquired the bounty of life from the earth and could have helped Lazarus. The rich man was responsible for helping the poor man laid at the gate of his life. Who is laid at the gate of your life?

Then I told my powerless Kenyan friends that the only reason the rich man was in Hades is because he did not help the poor man. To my surprise they leaped to their feet, lifted their hands, tears rolled down their cheeks.

My poor Kenyan friends understood. It was a number of years ago when this event occurred; to the best of my memory they continued their spontaneous outburst of praise and prayer for around twenty minutes.

On a trip to the Philippines, I was working with some old friends, Ray Nemenzo and James Balista in Cebu, Philippines. Ray faithfully taught, prayed with, and sought help for a large number of people known as 'scavengers'. These people lived and worked at the Lapu-Lapu city dumpsite. I taught the people at the dumpsite and wept over the despicable inhumane conditions they suffered.

Later in the week my friend Pastor James asked me if I wanted to speak for a local group of wealthy Filipinos that held church in a movie theater inside a mall.

I decided to instruct them on Jesus' teaching from the story of the Rich Man and Lazarus. I re-told Jesus' story in a manner that any person familiar with it would know, I was re-telling it.

There was once a wealthy Filipino. He lived in a beautiful house with blooming flowers and you could see his flat screen through his living room window. His home was protected from the violence of the outside world by a large concrete wall with broken glass along the top of the wall. He drove one of the finest cars in the city. When he would come home to his family in the evening he would push the gate opener as he drove into the security of his home. Each night as the rich Filipino man pushed the remote button to enter his property, the poor man was there, laid at his gate.

Poverty in the Philippines is everywhere; poor people suffering are an everyday sight that is treated as normal. A long day at the office, lots of challenges, so he closes his eyes to the immobile man laid at the gate of his life. He wants to hug his wife and children, enjoy a movie, eat some fine food, remove his suit and put on some comfortable clothes.

The next day as the rich Filipino man came home he noticed some commotion near his gate. A group of people was lifting the lifeless body of the poor beggar from the hedge outside the rich Filipino man's walled property. "So sad," he thought, "so sad; where is God to help all these poor people?"

I continued: Living in a world of poverty we find ourselves unable to respond as individuals to every need that we see. Yet, we must learn to identify the responsibility for the poor that has been laid at the gate of our lives. At the very least we all share in the responsibility to speak up for the cause of the poor and oppressed peoples of the world. I think Jesus expects each of us to identify and respond to the need of those that are laid at the gate of our life. The powerful are responsible for helping the poor. The status quo is unacceptable. We must never let our hearts grow callous to the suffering of other human beings; they are our brothers and sisters. There is one humanity, one family of God and we are all members. Our end is questioned in the story of the rich man and Lazarus.

The rich man's religious beliefs were incorrect, his wealth was blessing for all, not because of his heritage. His separation from inclusion as a child of Abraham was because of his failure to love the poor man who also was his brother. Love is personal and structural, the powerful cannot hide behind the systems of society and suppose their legal gain is acceptable; we often sacrifice our fellow human beings at the altar of progress. Wealth and power are for lifting up everyone around you. Your employees, your neighbors, are all laid at the gate of your life.

At the end of the service, all was quiet. My friend Pastor James brought me a sealed envelope filled with pesos. I gave it back to him so he could buy food for the children he fed on the streets of Cebu in the middle of the night. Every evening in Cebu the children of poor squatters came out to play on the manicured lawn of the capitol building. James was there feeding them. Every day people around the world scavenge in dumpsites. The world is filled with the children of Lazarus, the children of God.

Lightning and a Wild Man

The Personality and Story of Elijah

A mountain, lightning, fire, smoke, the earth shaking, and thick darkness - these are all indicative of the appearance of God (Ex 20:18; Ps 18). This display of earth shaking powers was present from Moses to Jesus' death. However, this physical display is not God, as Elijah will be told. The voice of God speaks in the soul like the shearing of silence and calls all unto his self.

Elijah liked a good show (1st Kings 17); his own appearance was a spectacle to behold. Elijah is easily recognized as a hairy man with a leather belt. His struggle with the spectacle of violence and feats of miraculous power followed him to the end of his life. The incredible life of the legendary immortal is a mixture of history, the extraordinary and the timelessness of myth. Knowing this, I am resistant to surrender all the extraordinary (miracles) to modern critical method.

When Elijah initially makes his appearance, he is neither a prophet nor a well-known figure. He is a wild man, a Nazarite, a zealous representative of monotheism (Yahweh). Elijah's abrupt appearance in the narrative of the kings is absent of a call narrative or any form of commissioning; both are common to the prophets. Although Elijah will move into the role of a prophet, he begins as a self-appointed religious zealot, driven by an uncommon personal faith that propels him into the public sphere of power to establish monotheism.

Elijah is set in contrast to two groups of people. The first group is Ahab and Jezebel. Ahab uses religion in compromising ways to maintain economic success and peace with his more powerful neighbors. Jezebel is the representative of foreign influence and epitomizes wickedness. The second group is the unnamed widow of Zarephath and Obadiah, who works to preserve Yahwist monotheism within the divergent religo-political powers. In contrast to Elijah, Ahab and Jezebel, both the widow and Obadiah preserve life: the widow feeds Elijah and Obadiah saves the lives of the Yahwist Prophets. For most of human history, the separation of state and religion was incomprehensible. This is the world where Elijah pursues his effort to prove God is one.[65]

---

[65] The abrupt appearance of Elijah and his ability to gain an audience with Ahab needs some comment. I do not think Elijah has a prior history as a prophet. Nor do I think his oath (As the LORD the God of Israel lives) followed by his self-positioning (before whom I stand) denotes access to the heavenly council. Elijah's monotheism is not compatible with the concept of a heavenly council, nor does Elijah

Elijah does not view reality with the same critical awareness of the prophets. The prophets view drought as God's work accomplished through the created order, where the ethical and moral behavior of humanity affects the physical world. Elijah's perspective is that the drought is a sign of punishment and is meant to turn King Ahab from syncretistic religious practices and end the worship of Baal. Further, the drought is brought on by Elijah's faith and supported by Elijah's oath, which draws Yahweh into the mix. The cast of characters is comprised of two groups of people caught up in the self-interjecting personality of Elijah and his unwavering conviction carried in a person whose exposure to 'others' has been limited, and whose personal growth is in need of some social maturation.

Elijah's willingness to challenge God and Ahab with the boldness of faith reflects a person who's on-the-job training is revealing of the relationship between God and Elijah. Elijah, like a minimally educated war strategist, knows that defeating an enemy is as simple as controlling the water supply. He lives with a constant awareness of God and his conviction runs so deeply that he initiates a showdown between his God and the pagan deity Baal. After his proclamation of a drought whose end is dependent upon his word, Elijah disappears and King Ahab cannot find him. Elijah has fled for his life and his uncompromising stance needs time. If he stays his life would surely be taken, or as Obadiah would later say, "The Spirit of Yahweh will carry you I know not where" (1st Kings 18:12).

---

report a heavenly vision. Elijah proclaims his own word based upon an oath and his way of living before God as a Nazarite. Elijah's appearance before Ahab is as intuitively providential as the drought he proclaims; without God, Elijah would be alone.

As a person, Elijah's view of reality is limited to his persona. He is a person of extremes. Elijah's appearance is carnivalesque; his personal emotions rise to heights of valiant expression and fall to lows where despair drives him to long for death. As a character, Elijah is void of family; he is a loner and his independent nature is in need of personal interaction. This need for personal interaction is primarily filled by Elijah's time with the widow of Zarephath.

After his announcement to Ahab, Elijah flees to the wilderness to hide, believing this is the will of God for him. The length of his stay is not defined but possibly it was only two days, the day he arrived and the day he left. The urgency depicted in this fast-paced narrative suggests that God's immediate response to Elijah is also desperate. What is God to do with this person whose faith has declared God to be alive and challenged the imperial power of Ahab? Elijah's education depicts a person who understands God as more of a singular nature God than a moral and ethical being, interested in educating humanity and revealing God's self in concert with said education.

Elijah's faith, his raw acceptance of leftover carrion from wild birds, finds God as the source rather than reducing his plight to desperation. In hiding, Elijah eats the unclean carrion of ravens and drinks water from a place where rainfall flows. Elijah's appetite must be satisfied; fasting is not an option. He is not seeking God in the wilderness, but survival. The omniscient narrator places Elijah's actions under the 'command' of God.[66] The

---

[66] The biblical narrators write from an 'all knowing' position as though they know the thoughts of both God and the characters of the stories they preserve.

only voice Elijah can discern is his own, which is that of a wild survivalist. And for Elijah, this is interpreted as God's voice. However, God has other plans and once the drought has begun taking effect, God sends Elijah to learn in the house of a widow.

Failed Education in the School of the Widow

Elijah, like a phoenix from ashes (not fire), rises from Israel's religious identity as a force of nature. Elijah is an earthy man who has more in common with Samson than he does with Moses. The remarkable aspect of Elijah as a person is his faith, not his courage that vacillates with his despairing temperament. Elijah is more of a sign than a prophet, more of an expressed need in its most primal form than an example. Israel as a people needs to believe! Unfortunately, they are a wild people with occasional bursts of faith in the Nazarite tradition and lack Torah as instruction in both the court of the king and in everyday life.

The Wildman, the hairy survivalist, the self-appointed prophet, the sign of need… needs education himself. Elijah has nowhere to go to learn Torah, so God has chosen a widow to be Elijah's teacher. Elijah has been informed that God has spoken to a widow and 'commanded' her to feed him. Elijah lacks any theological grounding, he writes nothing and his story is (like Samson's) flavored with the trappings of a dime novel from the old west.

When Elijah arrives in Zarephath the widow recognizes him and taunts him with his own oath formula (as Yahweh lives); however, she expresses her complete desperation and in the use of 'your God' differentiates her understanding of Yahweh from Elijah's. The God of the widow doesn't bring droughts to topple kings and leave widows to suffer. Her God cares for widows and sends Elijah to take care of her, so that she may feed him. The text sets forth the care of the widow in typical legendary discourse to magnify the person of Elijah.

We are never told how the widow's jars remained full; we are led to believe it was always miraculous. Of course, in a time of drought and famine it must have been, day by day, miraculous for a desperate widow and a fugitive zealot to have their needs met. I do not think we are to imagine Elijah spending three years in his upper room and hiding while the jars remained full. Rather, Elijah must survive by caring for the widow and her house. Elijah's strength and athletic adrenaline must serve the widow.

The widow of Zarephath is nameless, even as Elijah did not consider her when he stood before Yahweh, challenged Ahab, and declared a drought that would end only at his word. Only the raw, underdeveloped character of a wilderness survivalist matches the chutzpah of Elijah. The self-sufficient loner is admirable for his belief but is not an example to follow as a human being. Elijah's reputation as a miracle worker overshadows any sign of someone who cares about other human beings. Elijah cares only for the supremacy of his God, a God whom he experiences but fails to recognize along the way in the lives of the widow of Zarephath and Obadiah.

Elijah is a liminal person, disconnected from society, uneducated and untamed. Elijah does not recognize the faith of Obadiah or the widow; he considers himself to be alone when other believers in Yahweh have believed at the risk of losing their lives and been saved by the wisdom of Obadiah. Elijah doesn't know the 'seven thousand ' souls that have not bowed down to Baal, he doesn't even acknowledge their existence; he is alone.

The son of the widow of Zarephath becomes ill; her response reveals her displeasure with Elijah. It is apparent that the widow and Elijah have a less than exemplary relationship. He lives in her home as a dysfunctional liminal person, unable to adjust to the life of 'widows', of everyday people. This is so because Elijah never changes course in his perspective on how he is to live in relation to the consequences of his actions. Ultimately, Elijah's actions lead to his violent death.

The widow thinks of Elijah as an unforgiving, merciless character, disconnected from her reality. The cause of her son's illness is, in her thought, the result of living with this man who has no sympathy for widows. He has reminded her of her sins (1st Kings 17:18). We are not told what sin or sins that the widow recalls. I suspect the introduction of her son is a literary clue. Without a husband to care for her, she has either resorted to using her desirability as a female to gain the aid of a man or has prostituted herself. Possibly her son is not the child of her deceased husband. Elijah resorts to the power of his faith and heals the boy.

Elijah was given an opportunity by Yahweh to live with a woman, get to know her and possibly to have a family. Elijah's way of living and his concept of God leave widows helpless in a world of male dominance. Elijah is a man without responsibility and his zealousness is problematic for all, even God. However, God honors faith and works with all kinds of people, people like the widow, like Obadiah, and even like the miracle-working Elijah.

God sent Elijah to the widow to recognize the failure of his king-challenging fiasco that led to his flight into the wilderness where there was no manna, no quail, only the carrion of ravens. Elijah does not recognize his failure to fast and seek God's guidance. Elijah's trek to Horeb is in imitation of Moses and once again Elijah fails. Elijah does not receive a revelation of God but is rebuked for thinking God is a nature God that is known through acts of power. God attempts to teach Elijah that he speaks in the sheering silence of the soul where only God can be heard. God speaks in the heart of a widow who experiences the rash faith of Elijah as the cause of her suffering. God speaks in the life of Obadiah who saves Yahweh's prophets from Jezebel.

Elijah is a showman, a man of violence, and an uncompromising zealot unable to hear the voice of God. These loud, boisterous personalities show up often in religious circles. Their lives do not end well and neither does Elijah's (contrary to legend). The miracles in Elijah's life draw attention to his resolute faith, but the violence that follows his life distorts the revelation of God. This is readily demonstrable in the showdown orchestrated by Elijah, the carnivalesque showman.

Prior to focusing on Elijah's showdown with the prophets of Baal, it is important to view Elijah's slaughter of said prophets as his zealousness and identification with the history of zealot behavior established by Phinehas. Elijah was doing well until he succumbed to the violent tactics of his opponents. Nonetheless, Elijah calls fire (lightning) down from heaven. This event was the momentary eclipse of Baalism that tempted Elijah to end the threat of paganism. Elijah chose to strike with an act of terror into the heart of Baal worship (the slaughter of the prophets of Baal). The text leaves the reader with the impression that it was by Elijah's own hand that the prophets of Baal were all slain.

Elijah's uncompromising faith, driven by his own zealousness to see God in the world, produced miraculous signs that proved insufficient to bring change. Elijah followed his signs with acts of violence that are incompatible with the God who speaks into the souls of human beings. The immortal struggle of religious dedication to succumb to violence is, for those who hear the voice that shears the silence, ended on a cross, followed by an empty tomb.

My son insists, and I agree with him, that the only encouragement or advice that Moses and Elijah could offer Jesus at the transfiguration was not to fail as they had done through the use of anger or violence. Specifically, striking a rock or killing persons of errant belief. In the end, the 'chariots of Israel' in the blazing fire of an all out attack on Elijah ended his life. The legend makes his death a miraculous ascent; the truth sets aside the legend.

Jesus and Miracle Workers (Luke 4)

"Truly I tell you, no prophet is accepted in the prophet's hometown.
But the truth is, there were many widows in Israel in the time of Elijah,
when the heaven was shut up three years and six months, and there was a severe famine over all the land;
yet Elijah was sent to none of them except to a widow at Zarephath in Sidon.
There were also many lepers in Israel in the time of the prophet Elisha,
and none of them was cleansed except Naaman the Syrian."
(Luke 4:24-27)

After the temptations proffered by Satan to use power, and a ministry tour of Galilee, Jesus arrives in his hometown of Nazareth. It is likely that the stories about Jesus that had reached Nazareth carried the typical extrapolations of word of mouth news. It appears the people of Nazareth are expecting a prophet and miracle worker like Elijah and Elisha. Jesus is not interested in using power and violence to fight for deliverance from empire.

Jesus brings deliverance of a more immediate and personal nature by healing the broken bodies of those that have faith. Yet, Jesus will point to the power of their individual faith as the reason for their healing. Still, it is the identification of Jesus as a prophet that rests upon receiving healing. In Nazareth they will not recognize Jesus' teaching; they do not receive his role as a prophet, as one who speaks for God. They are expecting deliverance from Roman subjugation through violent prophets and a messianic King like David.

Jesus' responds with stories taken from the Elijah and Elisha narrative. Jesus is not interested in the acts of power that Elijah and Elisha are known for - acts over nature and violence against others. Rather, Jesus is interested in healing that results from the faith of a person who recognizes when God speaks. It is the faith of Elijah's widow and a leprous Syrian general that Jesus uses as positive examples.

The widow is a victim of Elijah's power and the Syrian General is an enemy of Israel. These two characters, the widow and Naaman, represent the universal aspect of Jesus' ministry to persons not recognized in Israel. They are examples of faith for recognizing Elijah and Elisha as prophets; even though they were of a lesser character than Jesus. Jesus is not like Elijah or Elisha.

It seems that miracles belong to a realm of experience that is inconsistent with day-to-day reality. Familiarity breaks down the relationship of the miracle worker with those who feel a landed connection with him or her. Miracles are easily forgotten, unable to produce faith, and require the unfamiliar. Jesus is more than a miracle worker and associates his ministry with the humility of the widow and Naaman, rather than with Elijah or Elisha.

Jesus exalts the ministry of Elijah and Elisha only in relation to their role in the life of the widow and the foreigner (even a leprous enemy general). Elijah and Elisha were celebrated among the populace. Jesus rejects celebrating his presence in relation to miraculous signs (John 4:48, Matthew 7:21-23). The miracle-working prophets fail as examples of faith in relation to their acts of power. The cause for celebration is the faith of the widow and the foreigner.

A Story of Raw Faith

Earthquake

Mike and Nympha 1976

When I write and share some of my stories I often experience deep-seated reluctance. This is so because my stories are a result of my choices and my life, which is but one amongst the myriads of human beings who have lived and died. I am sure that God watches the unfolding drama of humanity each day and is ever seeking signs of faith mixed in with the struggles of being human. The raw personality holding to faith with unwavering conviction often matures into a different person than when their journey began. Such persons possess a faith that brings God into the world and are unfamiliar with a world where God is silent, or where nature replaces God.

Prior to the day of the earthquake - the day that set my life firmly in place and affirmed my choice to be God's choice - was a series of profound experiences where God touched hearts on my behalf and honored my faith with favor. It is this series of events that make the earthquake more than chance, and so it became a pivotal moment in my faith development. The entire event is built around experiences that occurred while I was a young man in the Marines, a young man appalled by the abuse of power evident in the exploitation of the Filipina and the Philippines.

All naivety about the benevolent goodness of humanity existing within structures of legitimized violence was lost in a moment as I walked the streets of Olongapo. The systemic abuse of young women to relieve the sexual appetite of young and old soldiers was not representative of my concept of American virtue. The harsh contrast of wealth and poverty was an intolerable injustice.

After three sleepless nights of wrestling with both myself and the silence of God, I chose to marry a Filipina girl. Once I made this decision God's silence ended and my faith brought God into the world. Initially, I had to obtain approval from the U.S. military to marry Nympha, which was normally a six-month process. After a bold walk into the base commander's office, (curiously no one stopped me) I received permission three days later, through the military, to marry Trinidad (Nympha). The marriage approval process normally took six months.

After our wedding, I began the visa paperwork. I was told the process to obtain a visa normally took over a year. This was unacceptable for me and so with my raw faith, I moved forward.

My squadron was leaving to return to Okinawa and I received permission to remain in the Philippines on two-day rest and relaxation orders. My C.O. (commanding officer) told me to stay as long as I needed. It was nearly three weeks before I talked my way onto a C-130 to fly back to Okinawa. I had been suffering dysentery for a couple of months but I did not go to the infirmary because I knew they would keep me. I had experienced fever and blackouts but I kept going, believing God was with me (and watching).

It was a typical hot day in the Philippines and I had an appointment with the American Embassy to turn in my wife's visa application. My faith and determination to bring her home with me were immovable. We stood before a woman sitting at her desk. I placed the papers on her desk and asked when I could expect to have the visa approved. She informed me that I had married a foreigner and that it would be months before I heard from the embassy on the visa application. I informed her that I had married this woman and that I was going to bring her home with me. So, I asked if I could take the papers over to the foreign affairs office and to the labor department to be signed rather than wait for some bureaucrat to mail them across town.

She placed her hand on the papers and said, "Young man it is against the laaaaaa...." at that moment an earthquake shook the Embassy. The woman looked at me as if I was responsible for the earthquake and handed me the papers. I'm not sure why I wasn't surprised. Perhaps I had received enough divine favor from God through human beings that the extraordinary was closer to my experienced reality than at other times in my life. For me, this moment, the earthquake, makes believing that Elijah called down lightning an event within my own personal experience. Raw, innocent, uncomplicated faith ready to receive God into the world often belongs to people from the backwoods, the small community. I grew up in a small town near a condor sanctuary and spent a lot of time alone in the mountains and working an orange orchard. I had come face to face with a large cougar and numerous black bears and other wild creatures; I was not a city boy. I was a Pentecostal with a radical pursuit of God's Spirit melded into my religious training. In my faith, God acted on behalf of his servants who walk before him with faith, knowing that God is watching.

As a young man, I thought God had provided an earthquake solely for my wife and I. As I grew older I recognized the voice that silently shears the human heart had been at work in the people who helped me along the way. Today, I wrestle with the two: the power and the voice. Who God is can be hidden by acts of power, yet God longs for us to know who he is and to hear his voice. God's work brings into the world a peace that counters the ease of power reflected in the human propensity for violence.

I quickly took the papers from her hand and went across town to the foreign affairs office where I walked to the front of the line and asked to have the papers signed. Then I went to the Labor Department office, walked to the front of the line, paid a fee and had the appropriate papers signed. No one objected or questioned my actions when I walked past numbers of people to insist my papers be signed immediately. I returned to the U.S. embassy in Manila the same day. I talked my way in to see the woman who handed me the papers. When she saw me she asked how I had fared. I responded that I had the documents signed. She said "Great, when do you want to return and pick up your wife's visa?" I left that day with an appointment to pick up the visa on July 8th.

I returned to Okinawa for two weeks prior to flying back to the Philippines. This time I flew out of Okinawa with my American Passport. My orders were to take a military flight to Norton Air Force base in California.

I flew in at midnight, it was the era of Ferdinand Marcos' rule and martial law was in effect. I used an international traveler's pass, obtained at the airport, to travel at night to Subic. The taxi ride was a wild trip. The driver sped along the pothole-infested dirt road, desiring to make the trip as quickly as possible. Somewhere along the stretch through Pampanga a PNP (Philippine National Police) officer jumped out from the sugar cane with his shotgun pointed at us. The PNP officer was not familiar with an international traveler's pass and the conversation with the taxi driver was loud and intense. He eventually let us continue our journey to Olongapo City. My wife and I flew to the U.S. a few days later. One year later on, July 8th, our son was born.

CHAPTER IV

The Book of Proverbs and Relational Theology

The guiding mantra for living within the constraints of wisdom is 'fear of Yhwh. Although fear of Yhwh has many manifestations, it is ultimately a God - consciousness, an awareness of God at all times. Structurally the book of Proverbs builds upon the family as the place where wisdom is first encountered in a person's life.

> *The book of Proverbs recognizes both parents as*
> *purveyors of wisdom to their children.*
> *Hear, my child, your father's instruction,*
> *and do not reject your mother's teaching.*
> *Proverbs 1:8,9*

The inclusion of women in multiple literary strands and devices in Proverbs lends to a gender inclusive reading. In the verses above and below the poetic parallel lines place the importance of learning from both father and mother as synthetically equal. The translation of 'my son' as 'my child' is contextually legitimized.

> *My child, keep your father's commandment,*
> *and do not forsake your mother's teaching.*
> *Proverbs 6:20*

It is important to note that the first offering of wisdom is a piece on economics, justice, and the related desire for excess (1:10-19).

> *My child, if sinners entice you,*
> *do not consent.*
> *If they say, "Come with us, let us lie in wait for blood;*
> *let us wantonly ambush the innocent;*
> *like Sheol let us swallow them alive*
> *and whole, like those who go down to the Pit.*
> *We shall find all kinds of costly things;*
> *we shall fill our houses with booty.*
> *Throw in your lot among us;*
> *we will all have one purse" –*
> *my child, do not walk in their way,*
> *keep your foot from their paths;*
> *for their feet run to evil,*
> *and they hurry to shed blood.*
> *For in vain is the net baited*
> *while the bird is looking on;*
> *yet they lie in wait – to kill themselves!*
> *and set an ambush – for their own lives!*
> *Such is the end of all who are greedy for gain;*
> *it takes away the life of its possessors*

The warning is that a portion of humanity invites educated (wise) persons into a system of unjust gain. The cost of gain is portrayed as accomplished at the expense (the life and blood) of others. In the end, the power of money takes the life of its pursuer. In effect, money is a foreign power that overcomes the one who acquires wealth without justice.

The voice of wisdom is heard when 'fear of Yhwh' (an awareness that God is watching) is easily heard. To ignore the voice of wisdom is to court disruption of life and peace (1:20-33).

The voice of wisdom is the voice of Yhwh (2:6). The male in pursuit of wisdom is warned of the loose woman. Sexual restraint is training for the acquisition of wisdom and the successful life lived in the fear of Yhwh. The flow of wisdom (ideally) begins with learning from one's mother and father. At a basic level, wisdom begins with two immediate pieces of instruction; disdain greedy persons, and control your sexual impulses (this is so for both males and females).

Sexual Restraint

It is important to note the preceeding admonition for sexual restraint in the life of a male. Women captured in sexual promiscuity are (in the biblical text) considered to be victims of social constructs. This does not omit the occasional exception. For instance, Potiphar's wife, her motivation was directly related to the loss of power she experienced in relation to Joseph who was greater than her in Potiphar's house. The motivations of an adulteress are often about power and not love.

The sexual desire of human beings is not periodic like that of animals; it is continual, and as an impulse it must be trained. Wisdom is to embrace teaching on sexual restraint. Israel's first symbolic sign for male restraint is circumcision. In circumcision a male is made responsible for his 'seed' and the circumcision covenant with Yhwh is a constant reminder. Like their father Abraham, their lives are to model faith for their children after them. Circumcision demonstrates a covenant with Yhwh that takes control over the male's sexual activity and demands responsibility. The stories of Judah and his sons are about their failure and the ensuing consequences that result in the story of Tamar whose sexual impropriety is deemed 'more righteous'.

For moderns, circumcision as a religious act seems odd, disconnected, primitive. For Christians, it is (often) merely an unnecessary 'mutilation', except for health reasons. To reduce the act of circumcision to a 'health issue' is to miss the meaning behind the symbolic 'covenant-signing' act with all its instruction for human behavior. In particular, lessons in sexual restraint and male responsibility for human sexuality.

Male sexuality is governed by 'fear of Yhwh', accomplished through a covenantal symbolic sign. Female sexuality is governed by her desire for her husband and that governance is disrupted by social constructs. It is for this reason that Tamar is righteous and that the women in Hosea are not held accountable for their sexual behavior (Hosea 4:14).

The female desire for her husband is an underlying structure of reality. The theme of male responsibility is sewn into the fabric of reality. Romance, love, and a male are the ingredients for fulfilling a woman's right to have a child (or children). The woman naturally desires a male who will be faithful and responsible to her and 'their children'.

It is my thinking that males have more control of their sexuality than women, both inherently and sociologically; this is particularly so for the male of faith.

Women are naturally sensuous; meaning they have a strong aesthetic drive. The aesthetic is at the center of female thought processes (Gen. 3:6). The sensuousness of women is also built into their body and empowers them in the sight of the physically stronger male. Sensuousness has both positive and negative impact upon women. The negative is the tendency to anxiety; the positive is the need for 'spirit' that leads to the pursuit of God. It is faith that determines the impact of sensuousness upon the individual woman, whether negative or positive.

Wisdom is a Liberated Female

The personification of wisdom as a female links women to wisdom and makes wisdom desirable for traits that do not include sexuality. Proverbs 3:13-18 subtly associates the pursuit of wisdom with the pursuit of a woman who is focused on life and economic goals for security, yet she is to be understood as more valuable than any form of wealth.

The portrayal of wisdom as a female inspires young men to see in wisdom the sensuousness likened to the sensuousness of a woman. This equating of the feminine with wisdom balances the male tendency for domination. Wisdom is a power that is acquired by 'the fear of Yhwh', and it is the fear of Yhwh that teaches a man to desire a woman possessing the finer traits of faith exhibited in acts of compassion, love, and stability, these become the sensuous attraction that appeals to the male.

The Strange Woman

The fifth chapter of Proverbs is primarily about enforcing the effort to make a wise decision when choosing a woman. The loose 'strange' woman is pure sensuousness and void of wisdom (Proverbs 9:13-18). A strange woman is one who does not know how to live in harmony with the voice of wisdom in the world. She is void of faith, of the fear of YHWH.

The need to teach males sexual restraint is imperative for a healthy society. This being said, the use of negative female images is not an inappropriate metaphor to be viewed as detrimental to the well-being of women. The same type of critique is set against the unfaithful man who is equated with wickedness for not restraining his sexual impulse (Proverbs 5:20, 22). It is the male responsibility for structuring society in a healthy way that liberates women.

Excursus

You cannot legislate morality; meaning, legislation cannot change the heart (e.g. Josiah's reforms 2nd Kings 23). You can regulate behavior - with laws written to limit the damage of human immorality through fines and punishment that aid in preserving a moral society. Social structure forms human behavior; meaning institutional and cultural structures built upon law become unquestioned modes of living in society and form human behavior. Good laws have the power to affect moral ideas, concepts, and belief.

Wisdom literature was written for the schooling of scribes. Scribes were responsible for writing the laws of the king in the A.N.E. and in Israel. The scribes of Israel understood the previous paragraph. Understanding the scribes helps us read their texts. This is so for both legislation and wisdom literature.

The Birth of Lady Wisdom

Proverbs 8

An Introduction

Proverbs chapter eight is the principle passage that personifies wisdom as a lady. The passage is placed between the seductive adulterous of chapter seven and the foolish woman of 9:13-18. Interestingly, the book of Proverbs closes with an acrostic poem of the ideal wife, (Proverbs 31:10-31). There is a resonant tension in Proverbs between male dominance and the exalting of the female personage as a picture of wisdom. The male is warned of the seductive woman, but the woman is not warned of the seductive man.

The Proverbs are addressed to the son and not to a daughter. This dominance is expressed even in the oracle of a mother to her princely son, her words are introduced as; (Proverbs 31:1) *The words of King Lemuel. An oracle that his mother taught him:*. The mother's words are introduced as the words of King Lemuel and she remains nameless. On the other hand, the words are the mother's and not King Lemuel's. To the credit of those who formed the collection of the book of Proverbs, the tension of patriarchal culture with the female personification of wisdom is maintained even to the end of the book by the acrostic poem of the ideal wife.

Wisdom's divine origin is the subject of 8:22-31. Wisdom is revealed as an essential part of the created order, so essential that she must precede creation. In verse 22 the NRSV translates *qanah* as 'created', while the NKJV translates *qanah* as 'possessed'. It is significant that the word *bara* 'create' in Genesis is not utilized here. Some would use the passage in Genesis 14:19 to substantiate the translation of *qanah* as 'creation'. However, the translation of *qanah* as 'possessed' works well for the blessing that Melchizedek pronounces on Abraham. Likewise, of the eighty uses of *qanah* in the MT, all carry the meaning of buying, acquiring, purchasing or possessing. The question of *created* or *possessed* is one of philosophical theology. If wisdom was created, then she has a starting point. If she has a specific beginning then she is not an attribute of God, rather she is a reality that exists only in God's relation to creation. If wisdom has a starting point then God existed prior to her creation without wisdom. That God possesses wisdom is not a claim that requires argument. When wisdom is understood as an attribute of God that is revealed in the order of creation, the next step to a metaphorical personification is born of necessity. Wisdom takes on a life of its own as it is witnessed by humanity. Being revealed in the created order and witnessed to by humanity, wisdom must be spoken of in metaphorical terms.

Wisdom as a personified metaphor allows us to communicate wisdom as a way of aligning oneself with God through wisdom, while remaining distant from God's person.

The personification allows for wisdom to be separated from God, allowing for a distance between God's wisdom and the available wisdom given to man. So through use of the metaphor, man may partake of wisdom that comes from God but only in relation to creation. God remains sovereign and is not reduced to a spiritual commodity available through wisdom. Proverbs 8:13 remind the reader to fear Yahweh, who hates evil. Wisdom becomes a metaphorical living entity that ultimately delights in humanity, (Proverbs 8:31).

A Theology on Lady Wisdom

The birth of Lady Wisdom is the imagination of God arriving at a moment of choice whereby he will bring into existence the creation.

Wisdom (literature) is the effort to discern the voice of God in the creation. Israel's wisdom books are not dependent upon Israel's history of salvation. The wisdom books stand apart as Torah, they spring forth from reality, as natural as the thought of a mind in search of God. In the book of Proverbs we are introduced to lady wisdom as the personification of an ordered reality, imagined in the thought of God.

The underlying structures of reality reveal the voice of lady wisdom and lady wisdom is the voice of God in the creation. This 'voice' is the external witness of God displayed in the creation. The internal witness is the moral conscience and lady wisdom is the external guide, aiding the moral conscience. The moral conscience is attentiveness to the image of God within us.

Finally, lady wisdom is an ethical voice for justice and righteousness in a complex world where things are not the way they are supposed to be. This is so because the voice of lady wisdom is harmonious with a moral world.

The presence of humanity on the earth is disjunctive and does not work with the natural world but 'dominates'. This power to dominate is destructive if not attentive to the connection of wisdom's voice and morality. Of God's creatures, only humanity has access to the voice of lady wisdom because humanity functions with insight; we seek to understand. Lady wisdom functions within the sensuousness of the world to call humanity to live as 'spirit'.

Wisdom's primary instruction is to teach us to maneuver through life successfully and in particular to do so by establishing a proper relationship with one another as male and female. Wisdom also teaches us to live in a way that values human life over profit, over national security and ethnic difference, and do so in the face of power and not relent. Wisdom is interested in developing healthy human beings prepared to enter society. Wisdom is interested in healthy families where human beings are first formed as ethical beings.

Wisdom Liberates Women

Proverbs 31

The woman of Proverbs 31 is not merely an ideal; rather, she is an archetype for the capacity of a woman to excel in all aspects of society and culture. First, she knows how to live in proper relationship to her husband, not as less than, but as an equal. She is capable and trustworthy. She trades in clothing and food. She employs other women to learn to be like her. She purchases land and puts the land to use. She watches over her health so that she can serve the poor with her wealth. Her anxiety is nullified by her industrious ways and she ensures that her family is prepared for the seasons. She is a teacher and instructs her family. She is invited to speak at the city gates where the seat of economic affairs and governing takes place.

The ending of Proverbs with this woman who educated her kingly son is fitting. This is so because the book of Proverbs is about the development of wise human beings and recognizes the wisdom and equality of women. It is a profound ending that denies the patriarchalism of the age.

The book of Proverbs is structured around concepts of wisdom, male sexual restraint, teaching wisdom as family function, living successfully in a world of domination, and the need to acquire wisdom from women. In this respect, the ending of Proverbs recognizes a world where men need feminine wisdom.

Chapter V

Living as Male and Female

*If we can learn to live together as male and female
in a way that fulfills the image of God in us,
free from all socio-cultural inequities, we will
experience the healing of the world.*

The human condition is such that the primary relationship of human order is fraught with conflict. We are social, sexual, relational beings and it is the sexual aspect that causes us the most duress, the most problems, the most unrestrained desire. Sexual restraint is a learned practice and can be a spiritual exercise.

The scripture is a witness to the failings of males in particular to live appropriately in relation to females. The male desire to possess the woman and the male tendency to violence fills the stories of scripture. The domination of the female is one of the greater sins of humanity. For this reason, a wise society will initiate laws to protect and equalize women.[67]

---

[67] The equalization of women in military service is problematic. The myth of the Amazonian warrior is opposed to all that constitutes the life of women. It is not that warring is natural for males, but part of the alleged purpose of warring is the appeal to the natural role of the male as protector of women and children based upon size, strength,

Sexual Restraint and Spirituality

In the scripture, at the heart of the meaning and practice of circumcision is sexual restraint. A male is to remember that as a child of Abraham, a recipient of an inherited promise, he is responsible to God for his offspring. In effect, the sexual behavior of the male Israelite belongs to God. A covenant sealed in the cutting of the flesh - the blood representing life - is the male's affirmation of the connectedness of life through procreation.

The story of Noah's drunken state and exposed sexual life with his wife when his 'youngest son' Canaan finds them in their tent is a lesson in the taboo of sexual exposure; sexuality is meant to be hidden (Gen. 9:20-27). Canaan's violation of the sexual privacy of his grandfather (or possible sexual assault) results in a curse from Noah. Noah's curse is more expressive of the repercussions of unrestrained aberrant sexual behavior than any power in Noah's speech. The story also advises soberness when engaging in sex and locking one's door.

The first couple, Adam and Eve, experiences the tension of their difference when Adam remains in silence during Eve's display of aesthetic, ethical and religious thought as she reasons over the forbidden fruit. The celebration of their gendered reality is lost to the desire for greatness, rather than submission to the limited realities of life as creatures in the garden of God. Adam desires to possess the woman, rather than be an equal partner in life. So, she reaches beyond the structures of reality expressing her

---

and the male as taker in contrast to the female as giver. The inclusion of women in military service is indicative of a loss of gender identity in society.

tendency towards anxiety and spirit. Adam succumbs to his wife's invitation to eat, for he desires the woman, more than the God who created him.

I have noted in this work that the book of Proverbs consistently calls for sexual restraint if a person is to achieve wisdom in the world or enduring success. I think Paul recognizes the prohibition on sexual intercourse during the menstrual cycle as a natural time for developing sexual restraint. However, Paul's view on the value of sexual restraint for the sake of spiritual control over one's self is not limited to the natural restraint during the menstrual cycle.

The need for food and the sexual impulse belong to the flesh. For this reason abstaining from either for the sake of spiritual development and self-control constitutes spirituality; this is so for both males and females. However, both food and sex are necessary for the continuance of life. Abstaining from either for prolonged periods of time is unwise; or as Paul would say it is better to marry than to burn; I'm sure he means burn with sexual passion.

Chapter VI

Relational Theology and the book of JOB

Polyphonic Depictions of Yahweh

The depictions of Yahweh in the book of Job are a reflection of humanity's assorted thoughts, experiences, and hopes. When forming theology from the book, it is important to read with the heart of a poet, to allow the aesthetic to mix with the ethical and let the religious melt into the reality of human experience. This is so because the entirety of the dialogues was written in Hebrew poetry. A literal reading, or a purely mechanical reading, will fail to draw the reader into the mosaic-vision and adventure of the writer searching for the Spirit with a story reflective of universal human reality and Hebraic culture.

A compassionate reading, with the suffering of humanity throughout the world's history kept in mind, should ignite the imagination of the reader when reading Job. I certainly appreciate the hermeneutical science of biblical study and have done my share of exegetical, grammatical, and historical work with the text. Yet, it is the poetic lens that is able to capture the depth of the book's many revelations. Truly the book of Job is a product of an unparalleled literary and theological genius; who was a poet and a playwright. The author of Job was a person deeply concerned with finding God, a person who knew that only a person free of guilt could speak in a manner befitting his needs as a writer and theologian. The author writes with honesty about reality that is seldom seen in religious writings; herein is his/her intelligence and spiritual tenacity.

One aspect of the book of Job is the depictions of the voices of Yahweh as portrayed in the prologue, dialogues, God speeches and epilogue. The book of Job displays how we relate to God through myth, transcendence, wealth, suffering, religious tradition, fear, hope and need are all pictured in the Joban narrative. This is the effort of this chapter to reveal the relational aspect of humanity and God through the portrayals of God in the book of Job.

The God of the Prologue

The book's maneuver to avoid the problem of evil is to assign it to the mythical use of a heavenly council and an adversarial figure (the satan) who questions God's admiration for Job.[68] However, Job accepts both good and evil as realities that proceed forth from God.[69]

> *But he said to her,*
> *"You speak as any foolish woman would speak. Shall we*
> *receive the good at the hand of God, and not receive the bad?"*
> *In all this Job did not sin with his lips.*
> *(Job 2:10)*

The folktale (Job 1-2) is presented as a conclusive unit on the story of Job. It serves as a literary device to provide

---

[68] I am fond of saying, "I have solved the problem of evil; said no one ever".

[69] The disconnect between the mythological folktale and the dialogues that are deeply embedded in human emotions and experience, serves the purpose of allowing transcendence into the book of Job. There is no answer for the question of how the author knew of the heavenly scene. This is so because the folktale belongs to the realm of the unknown. The folktale provides a subconscious lens for reading the dialogues of Job and his friends.

the reader with expectations of a story about a hero. The dialogues take the reader deeper into the struggles of being human. In the dialogues Job will not be so kind, for he knows nothing of other beings in heavenly realms. Rather, Job is a pure monotheist.

> *The earth is given into the hand of the wicked;*
> *he covers the eyes of its judges –*
> *if it is not he, who then is it?*
> *(Job 9:24)*

The author's use of the folk tale in the prologue with its mythical imaginative moment as the introduction to his literary work helps the reader move into the drama without entertaining the unanswerable problem of evil. It also sets the scene for setting up Job as the archetypal human being whose experiences cover the gamut of human suffering.[70]

> *The God in the folktale cannot be questioned*
> *for he lives in the realm of myth.*

The initial relationship in the book of Job is between God and Job. God is proud of Job; Job appeases God through pious practices. God can watch Job and Job believed God to be watching. However, the relationship is tenuous, there is no interaction or speech only God watching and Job believing he is being watched.

---

[70] See: Mike Garner, *Everyday Thoughts: A Collection of Devotional Readings for Thinking Christians,* (West Conshoshocken, PA: Infinity Publishing, 2015) pgs. 125-131. The book of Job is a reflection on the human condition in light of monotheism and freely links Job to Adam as a voice from a known reality over against the mythical garden. In a single verse, Job is linked to both Adam and the voice of wisdom (Job 15:7).

> *If I sin, what do I do to you, you watcher of humanity?*
> *Why have you made me your target?*
> *Why have I become a burden to you?*
> *(Job 7:20)*

The adversarial figure of 'the satan' appears only in the folk tale and will not be mentioned in any fashion throughout the entirety of the dialogues. Job's wife as a character is presented in a way that supports the effort to make Job the archetypal sufferer, a voice for all humanity. As the only person who should have stayed at his side, she abandons him after the natural disasters, warring raiders, the loss of his children and his health. Job's love for his children was displayed through his pious exercise of sacrifice.

Job's wife cannot reflect the ideal of a woman who stays by her husband's side; she must be presented as a person appalled by the man for whom she bore children. She must reflect the human reality of how we treat the suffering as 'cursed' in order to appease our own conscience. Job must experience abandonment, isolation, and be reduced to a person with only one power; speech. He must experience betrayal in the one relationship that he needed most. Only then can he become an archetype for all humanity.

This is the beginning of a contest between Job's experience of God and traditional beliefs. Job held the traditional view of his friends until suffering hit his life. Job's suffering is an extreme test. Job will become the voice of humanity. We learn from him that human experience is valid for theological speech when spoken in honesty with faith, even when accusation is turned upon God.

> *But he knows the way that I take;*
> *when he has tested me, I shall come out like gold.*
> *(Job 23:10)*

Mythical Men

Job's sole point of strength for surviving the terror that has engulfed him is confidence in his speech that is rooted in an integrous life. In this sense, Job replaces Adam as the archetypal human being. Job is without any consciousness of sin. This enables him to speak in ways that release him from the effects of guilt. Yet, Job has never known the garden of naivety where walks with God in the cool of the day were to be normative.[71] Job is like us; he lives in a world where the innocent suffer. The author, through the questioning of Job by Eliphaz, introduces the Joban narrative as a competing story with the Garden narrative on the human condition.

> *"Are you the firstborn of the human race?*
> *Were you brought forth before the hills?*
> *(Job 15:7)*

This is Eliphaz's perception of Job's speech. In the folktale God has confirmed that Job is (tam, yashar) blameless and upright. Job holds to his integrity. Job is the center of attention; he is the realized personification of human experience and suffering. Job is a matured man - once a sheik, once he had a wife and children, then he

---

[71] I provide a complete study on how the book of Job offers a competing story to the garden narrative in another work. See: Garner, Mike *Everyday Thoughts: A Collection of Devotional Readings for Thinking Christians,* (West Conshoshocken, PA: Infinity Publishing, 2015) pgs. 125-131.

experiences loss through both natural disaster and war - his flesh suffers some outbreak that indicates his blood is poisoned; Job is alone in the world. His friends (fellow sheiks) become his accusers. The local populace sees him as someone to scorn, for God has spoken (through the calamities) and Job must be guilty of heinous sins.

But Job is the hero of the story! He speaks for humanity as only he can. He speaks of the human condition outside of any doctrine on the fall of man or original sin. The book of Job is a competing story for understanding the human condition, this is so because Job the sufferer is an innocent victim of reality and embodies the finest theological wisdom of the era. The book of Job reveals that wisdom belongs to the suffering who are not blinded by wealth and power. After all, Job's wisdom would not be available to us were it not for his suffering. In this capacity, the book of Job is revelatory in relation to the coming of God into the world in Jesus.

The relationship to Job and the reader is his speech. His words resist the condemnation of guilt; youthful mischief cannot touch his conscience. He has not committed any sin that would account for the degree of his suffering. Although Job's belief in God is unremitting, God remains hidden behind the myth of an unquestionable heavenly realm for both Job and the reader.

The Almighty God of the Tradition

The god of the tradition is the god of the status quo. He is at the service of the powerful. He is a cultural god who affirms the righteous man with wealth, health, and power. The religious ideologies of the tradition are as unrealistic or unreasonable as the god they represent. Job's accusations expose the god of the tradition as unjust; his friends can only insist that Job is reaping what he has sown. The theology of the tradition is retributive and supports the status quo of the world.

Job's Despair

Job's first speech is a despairing rebuke to God over the extreme reality of human suffering. Job even seeks death, yet he will not take his own life. The mystery of the resiliency of the human spirit, the preciousness of life in spite of pain and suffering, is a repeated phenomenon in human history. Human beings have survived through unspeakable evil and suffering and survived to become exemplary human beings. In the recesses of Job's complaint lies a revealing truth: suffering often makes us better human beings. It is also true that those who suffer the most are usually the innocent.

Job's Relationship to his Fellow Sheiks

Job's friends always held in their power the ability to lift Job from the ashes, treat his sores, restore to him wealth and help him rebuild his home. Job the sufferer becomes Job the priest who speaks correctly about God. The restoration of Job's wealth seems to initially have taken place upon the completion of Job's prayer for his accusing friends - they gave more than sacrificial bulls to Job. People continued to give to Job once his vindication had begun.

It is notable that the archetypal sufferer, the voice for humanity, speaks truth about God and so others voluntarily make him wealthy. This part of the ending of Job portrays wisdom as alive in the world when suffering humanity is restored from the calamity of natural disaster, warring, illness, betrayal, abandonment, and marginalization. The healing of humanity, the practice of tikkun olam, and liberation theology find support in the books ending.

The God of Nature

It is helpful for the reader to imagine the Joban story as a performance, a script for a play. The setting of the scene when God speaks out of the whirlwind heightens the reader's senses for the climactic conclusion to Job's quest for the God he needs.

The poet is about to take his reader into a deadly storm where darkness and wind speak like Leviathan. The courage of our hero - who has continued to speak throughout the torturous experience of his life - a life set in the drama of history for the viewing of God and man, is now facing a vision of God that is merciless. His hope of bringing God into the court of human understanding is going to end, as is his speaking.

In the God speeches of chapters 38-41, Yahweh is perceived as a cruel, compassionless God. The poet has drawn upon our primal fears of a reality where the cosmos alone is the revelation of God. It is a dark picture of nature turned on destruction in a whirlwind. It was a windstorm that had taken the lives of Job's children as they were feasting in their eldest brother's house. Job has repeatedly asked God to allow him to plead his case before him without the fear and dread that would inhibit him from speaking. Now,

Job's mind wonders at the meaning of this wind; fear and dread fill his soul and the depiction of the voice from the whirlwind is an expression of humanity's experience of God's voice as the speech of nature.

Job has sought throughout the dialogues to bring God into the concrete reality of human experience, to remove God from the myth of transcendent inculpability. The absence of God is equatable with transcendent inculpability. God's absence (the watcher) is insufficient for the God who Job needs. Job's belief has carried him to the precipice of unmatched theological revelation during the dialogues.

1) Job views Sheol as a place from which God can hide and restore life. This piece also forms a chiasm built around the question of life after death. At the same time, the piece suggests that the soul can be restored from Sheol.

Oh that you would hide me in Sheol,
    that you would conceal me until your wrath is past,
        that you would appoint me a set time, and remember me!
            If mortals die, will they live again?
            All the days of my service I would wait until my release should come.
    You would call, and I would answer you;
you would long for the work of your hands.

(Job 14:13-15)

2) Job questions God's judgment of humanity based upon God's lack of human experience. In a sense this piece of Job's speech suggests that God must experience life as a mortal if God is

to judge humanity as one who understands the plight of human life.

Do you have eyes of flesh?
Do you see as humans see?
(Job 10:4)

3) The Joban author makes the cry of the sufferer's words of eternal concern. Job's deepest convictions are revealed: Job believes in a God of redemption, a God who can and will be seen; the God - who Job will meet on the day of justice when God is on the side of the suffering.

"O that my words were written down!
O that they were inscribed in a book!
O that with an iron pen and with lead
they were engraved on a rock forever!
For I know that my Redeemer lives,
and that at the last he will stand upon the earth;
and after my skin has been thus destroyed,
then in my flesh I shall see God,
whom I shall see on my side,
and my eyes shall behold, and not another.
My heart faints within me!
(Job 19:23)

Now, in this darkest of moments, will Job be swallowed up in the whirlwind? Job's responses are out of fear; his speech has come to an end. He will refuse to carry on with his case and upon dust and ashes he is left at the mercy of this God who speaks from out of the chaos. Job will not deliver the final word on human experience. The God Job needs is yet to be revealed.

My Translation:[72]

> *therefore I refuse,*
> *and change my mind upon dust and ashes."*
> *(Job 42:6)*

This incomplete contest with God and humanity will require further revelation to be found in the life of Jesus Christ the Lord. Yet the dialogue between God and humanity will continue as human beings seek for meaning and wrestle with the injustices and suffering that fill our lives. Job is exhausted but has not surrendered indefinitely; the pursuit for meaning will continue. However, Job has been tested to the core of his being and held to his integrity.

Job's speeches all seek a God who is not simply reflected in the created order or bound to the structures of reality. Job searches for the God who transcends the limits of creation. Job's theology is ontological and will not settle for the incoherence of myth, the irrational aspects of tradition, or the limits of creation as acceptable. Job searches for and needs a God who is more than a watcher. Job needs a God who respects humanity and engages in speech from a place of powerlessness.

---

[72] This verse to be translated correctly according to the MT must read 'I refuse' in spite of the absence of an object for the verb. Translators do not follow the text but change the verb to a reflexive 'I despise myself'. However it is clear within the context of the dialogue that Job is refusing to continue his effort to bring God into the court of human understanding. The verb translated as 'repent' in the second line I have translated as 'change my mind'. The verb is 'nahamti' and not the word repent, which is 'shub'. Job is not repenting but changing his mind in response to the frightening whirlwind and the accompanying theophany.

The God Who Cares

Now, Yahweh speaks and it is this depiction of Yahweh that is communicative for relationship with humanity, rather than merely a watcher. The speech is relational in a way that the God who cares finally speaks. The speech of God is directed towards the voices for the tradition; Job's fellow sheiks. They have apparently been present for the whirlwind theophany. Job alone had the courage to respond, even though fear and dread accompanied the moment. This is an amazing testament to the tenacity of Job. His friends had nothing to say, their theology was as much without character as they themselves were. Confronted by the ominous presence of Yahweh they are silent. Their silence is reflective of their speeches directed at Job. Their words were empty, unsupported by compassion or love for their friend. During the dialogues, Job often ignored the words of his fellow sheiks and spoke directly to God as though Yahweh was listening.[73] The silence motif in the dialogues comes to fruition at the moment of the theophany. The tradition had domesticated God and failed to produce servant-leaders like Job.

The God Job Needs

The God Job needs is found particularly in Job's theology, built from his hope and suffering. The God of the epilogue - the God who cares - is a partial picture of

---

[73] Although 'the name' Yahweh appears only once in the dialogues, it is this single appearance that affirms it is Yahweh that Job and his friends are speaking of and on behalf of. The absence of 'the name' in the dialogues allows for affirming the setting of the story as prior to the revelation of God at Sinai. The antiquity of the story allows for a universalizing of the term El for speaking about the one God.

that God whose purposes are yet to see the fulfillment of Job's hope and convictions. The God of Job's deepest conviction at the conclusion of ch. 19 is a redeeming God. He is also more than Job can breathe out in words; he is the unimaginable God of merciful justice and an incomprehensible resurrection.

Job's speeches are redeemed and the words of his friends renounced. Yahweh is not pleased with the friends and requires their submission to Job. Job has become their priest and he prays for his fellow sheiks.

The epilogue is brief and ends quickly. The restoration of Job occurs prior to the return of friends and family in verse 11. It seems that this restoration of fortune came from the source that was present from the beginning of the dialogues, which is from Job's fellow sheiks. They could have helped Job at the beginning but they chose to accuse him rather than restore his life. In this respect, the story of Job is similar to Jesus' parable of Lazarus and the rich man. The help that God had provided for Lazarus was in the power of the rich man who ignored poor Lazarus.

Traditional religion and the powerful often accuse those in need as irresponsible and deserving of their plight. The wealthy and powerful love religion that legitimizes their consumption and negates their responsibility as part of the human family.

Job's story concludes with a happy ending for our hero. Yet, Job experienced real loss in the death of his children. Likely the abandonment of his wife can be viewed as permanent. Job's wife is not mentioned in the list of returning friends and family found in the epilogue. The loss of Job's children is permanent, the estrangement from his wife severe. His restoration lacks the power of resurrection.

A glimpse of the God of Job's need, works on his behalf only in the epilogue. Jobs encounter with Yahweh is purest at the moment of his restoration from the testing he has endured. Yet it would be foolish to think that life always ends on a happy note for the righteous. Our faith and hope abide with love for God through the mess that is human life. Every story has its limits for application to life. The book of Job teaches us that it is the view of reality held by the suffering that exposes the failings of tradition.

The polyphonic voice of God in the Joban text are each a part of our perception in the search for God. We view God through myth, through tradition, through nature, and yet through religion hope for a God whose love is unfathomable and whose power returns the dead. We hope for a God who cares and need a God we have not yet seen in history. In Christ Jesus this has changed, yet the consummation of the revelation of God in Christ Jesus is yet to be completed as the final act.

Job's Daughters

Job knows that women and children suffer just like men. He leaves his daughters an inheritance and by doing so affirms that he opposes a world where women are not equal to men. This is a fitting way to end a book in search of wisdom, in search of God. The violence done to women through patriarchy is rejected after Job's suffering has re-educated him to human reality. The God of the tradition is no longer Job's God. Job's God is the God of suffering humanity, a watcher, a redeemer; and his progressive revelation in human history continues in the battle of words for talking about God.

Conclusion

In the book of Job there are five distinct experiences of God depicted: 1) the transcendent through myth 2) the traditional God who supports the status quo 3) the fearsome God of chaos 4) the God who cares 5) and the God whom Job needs. It is the God who cares that requires Job's restoration at the expense of his friends.

The vision of God that possesses Job is the God whom Job needs. Ultimately the God that Job needs is yet to come, yet to tabernacle in flesh and experience being human, yet to appear among us free from inhibiting speech with fear and dread; he is yet to appear as the one who calls us forth from Sheol and stands at our side as our redeemer. Job's hope for the God he needs is, in a sense, a depiction of the Lord to come - the one who has eyes like Job, the one who unites God and human experience in a single Lord.

yet for us there is one God,
the Father, from whom are all things and for whom
we exist, and one Lord, Jesus Christ, through whom
are all things and through whom we exist.
(1st Corinthians 8:6)

BIBLIOGRAPHY

Badiou, Alan. *Saint Paul: The Foundation of Universalism.* Palo Alto, CA: Stanford University Press, 2003.

Bellinger, Charles K. *The Genealogy of Violence: Reflections on Creation, Freedom, and Evil.* New York: Oxford University Press, 2001.

Berrigan, Daniel *To Dwell in Peace: An Autobiography.* New York: Harper and Row, 1987.

Burke, Kevin F., and Robert Lassalle-Klein, eds. *Love that Produces Hope: The Thought of Igancio Ellacuria.* Collegeville, MN: Liturgical Press, 2006.

Childs, Brevards S. *Myth and Reality in the Old Testament.* London: SCM Press, 1962. Ed. Botta, Alejandro F. and Andinach, Pablo R. *The Bible and the Hermeneutics of Liberation.* Atlanta, GA. SBL, 2009.

Freire, Paulo. *Pedagagy of Freedom: Ethics, Democracy and Civic Courage* . Translated by Patrick Clarke. Lanham, MD: Rowman and Littlefield Publishers, 1998.

Garner, Mike *Interpretive Adventures; Subversive Readings in a Missional School*, West Conshoshocken, PA: Infinity Publishing, 2015.

Garner, Mike *Everyday Thoughts: A Collection of Devotional Readings for Thinking Christians*. West Conshoshocken, PA: Infinity Publishing, 2015.

Gill, Lesley *The School of the Americas: Military Training and Political Violence in the Americas,* Durham, NC: Duke University Press, 2004.

Hartley, John E. *The Book of Job.* New International Commentary on the Old Testament. Grand Rapids, Michigan: Eerdmans, 1988.

Heschel, Abraham Joshua. *Moral Grandeur and Spiritual Audacity.* U.S.A.: Farrar, Straud and Giroux, 1996.

Iriye, Akira. *The Origins of the Second World War in Asia and the Pacific.* London, England: Longman Group, 1987.

Kierkegaard, Søren, Reidar Thomte, and Albert Anderson. *The Concept of Anxiety: A simple psychologically orienting deliberation on the dogmatic issue of hereditary sin.* Princeton, N.J.: Princeton University Press, 1980.

Linn, Brian McAllister. *The Phillipine War 1899-1902.* Lawerence, Kansas: University Press of Kansas, 2000.

Millgram, Hillel. *The Elijah Enigma: The Prophet, King Ahab and the Rebirth of Monotheism in Israel.* Jefferson NC: MacFarland Publishing, 2014.

Newsom, Carol A. *The Book of Job: A Contest of Moral Imaginations.* Oxford NY: Oxford University Press, 2003.

Olson, Dennis T. *Deuteronomy and the Death of Moses: A Theological Reading.* Minneapolis, MN: Augsburg Fortress Press, 1999.

Pritchard, James B. *Ancient Near Eastern Texts Relating to the Old Testament.* 3rd ed. Princeton: Princeton University Press, 1969.

Redekop, Calvin W. *Mennonite Entrepreneurs: (Center Books in Anabaptist Studies).*

Baltimore, MA: John Hopkins University Press, 1995.

Ruden, Sarah *Paul Among the People: The Apostle Reinterpreted and Reimagined in His Own Time.* New York: Random House Publishers, 2010.

San Juan Jr., E. *The Philippine Temptation: Dialectics of Philippines--U.S. Literary Relations.* Philadelphia PA. Temple University Press, 1996.

Scott, James C. *The Moral Economy of the Peasant: Rebellion and Subsistence in Southeast Asia.* London, England: Yale University Press, 1976.

Vine, David *Base Nation: How U.S. Military Bases Abroad Harm America and the World.* New York: Metropolitan Books, 2015.

Wellborn, L.L. Politics and Rhetoric in the Corinthian Epistles. Macon, Georgia: Mercer University Press, 1997

Zornberg, Avivah Gottlieb. *Bewilderments: Reflections on the Book of Numbers.* New York: Schocken Books, 2015.

www.ingramcontent.com/pod-product-compliance
Lightning Source LLC
Chambersburg PA
CBHW050345230426
43663CB00010B/2003